Building Moderate Muslim Networks

Angel Rabasa
Cheryl Benard
Lowell H. Schwartz
Peter Sickle

Sponsored by the Smith Richardson Foundation

 CENTER FOR MIDDLE EAST PUBLIC POLICY

BP163
B745

The research described in this report was sponsored by the Smith Richardson Foundation and was conducted under the auspices of the RAND Center for Middle East Public Policy.

Library of Congress Cataloging-in-Publication Data

Building moderate Muslim networks / Angel Rabasa, Cheryl Benard,
    Lowell H. Schwartz, Peter Sickle.
        p. cm.
    Includes bibliographical references.
    ISBN 978-0-8330-4122-7 (pbk. : alk. paper)
    1. Islam—21st century. 2. Islamic fundamentalism. 3. Islamic countries—
Relations—United States. 4. United States—Relations—Islamic countries. I.
Rabasa, Angel.

BP163.B745 2007
320.5'57090511—dc22

                                                                    2006101898

The RAND Corporation is a nonprofit research organization providing objective analysis and effective solutions that address the challenges facing the public and private sectors around the world. RAND's publications do not necessarily reflect the opinions of its research clients and sponsors.

RAND® is a registered trademark.

Cover design by Eileen Delson La Russo

Published 2007 by the RAND Corporation
1776 Main Street, P.O. Box 2138, Santa Monica, CA 90407-2138
1200 South Hayes Street, Arlington, VA 22202-5050
4570 Fifth Avenue, Suite 600, Pittsburgh, PA 15213-2665
RAND URL: http://www.rand.org/
To order RAND documents or to obtain additional information, contact
Distribution Services: Telephone: (310) 451-7002;
Fax: (310) 451-6915; Email: order@rand.org

Preface

The struggle underway throughout much of the Muslim world is essentially a war of ideas. Its outcome will determine the future direction of the Muslim world and whether the threat of jihadist terrorism continues, with some Muslim societies falling back even further into patterns of intolerance and violence. It profoundly affects the security of the West. While radical Islamists are a minority almost everywhere, in many areas they hold the advantage. To a large extent, this is because they have developed extensive networks spanning the Muslim world and sometimes reaching beyond it, to Muslim communities in North America and Europe. Moderate and liberal Muslims, although a majority in most Muslim countries and communities, have not created similar networks. Moderate Muslim networks and institutions would provide a platform to amplify the message of moderate as well as some measure of protection from violence and intimidation.

Moderates, however, do not have the resources to create these networks themselves; they may require an external catalyst. With considerable experience dating back to the U.S. efforts during the Cold War to foster networks of people committed to free and democratic ideas, the United States has a critical role to play in leveling the playing field for moderates. What is needed at this stage is to derive lessons from the experience of the Cold War, determine their applicability to the conditions of the Muslim world today, and develop a "road map" for the construction of moderate and liberal Muslim networks—what this study proposes to do.

The research behind this monograph builds on the RAND Corporation's previous work on moderate Islam, particularly Angel Rabasa et al., *The Muslim World After 9/11*, and Cheryl Benard, *Civil Democratic Islam*. Funded by a grant from the Smith Richardson Foundation, this research was conducted within the RAND Center for Middle East Public Policy (CMEPP). CMEPP is part of International Programs at the RAND Corporation, which aims to improve public policy by providing decisionmakers and the public with rigorous, objective research on critical policy issues affecting the Middle East.

Addressing one of the central issues of our time—the war of ideas within Islam—this study is germane to the strategic interests of the United States and its allies and is directly related to the Smith Richardson Foundation's view that the United States continues to face the challenge of enhancing international order and advancing U.S. interests and values abroad. This monograph should be of value to the national security community and interested members of the general public, both in the United States and abroad. Comments are welcome and should be addressed to the authors:

Dr. Angel M. Rabasa   Dr. Cheryl Benard
RAND Corporation   RAND Corporation
1200 South Hayes Street   1200 South Hayes Street
Arlington, Virginia 22202   Arlington, Virginia 22202
rabasa@rand.org   benard@rand.org

For more information on the RAND Center for Middle East Public Policy, contact the Director, David Aaron. He can be reached by e-mail at David_Aaron@rand.org or by mail at RAND, 1776 Main Street, Santa Monica, California 90407-2138. For information on RAND's International Programs, contact the Director, Susan Everingham at Susan_Everingham@rand.org or by mail at RAND's Corporate Headquarters in Santa Monica. More information about the RAND Corporation is available at www.rand.org.

Contents

Preface iii

Figure and Tables ix

Summary xi

Acknowledgments xxv

Abbreviations xxix

CHAPTER ONE

Introduction 1

The Challenge of Radical Islam 1

Potential Partners and Allies 3

CHAPTER TWO

The Cold War Experience 7

U.S. Grand Strategy at the Beginning of the Cold War 7

Political Warfare 10

U.S. Networking Efforts 13

    Liberation Committees 14

    Congress of Cultural Freedom 18

    Labor Unions 22

    Student Organizations 24

    Role of U.S. Government Foundation-Like 26

British Network-Building Activities 29

Lessons from the Cold War Experience 30

Why Was the Effort Successful? 33

CHAPTER THREE
Parallels Between the Cold War and the Challenges in the Muslim World Today 35

CHAPTER FOUR
U.S. Government Efforts to Stem the Radical Tide 41
U.S. Government Programs and Challenges for the Future 43
Democracy Promotion 44
Civil-Society Development 49
Public Diplomacy 54
Case Study: The Middle East Partnership Initiative 57
The BMENA Foundation for the Future 61
Conclusions 63

CHAPTER FIVE
Road Map for Moderate Network Building in the Muslim World 65
Identifying Key Partners and Audiences 65
Characteristics of Moderate Muslims 66
    Democracy 66
    Acceptance of Nonsectarian Sources of Law 67
    Respect for the Rights of Women and Religious Minorities 67
    Opposition to Terrorism and Illegitimate Violence 68
Application of Criteria 68
Potential Partners 70
    Secularists 70
    Liberal Muslims 71
    Moderate Traditionalists and Sufis 73
Should Islamists Be Engaged? 75
Delivering Support to Moderates 78
    Partners 79
    Programmatic Priorities 81
    Regional Focus 84
Obstacles to a Regional Approach 87
The Role of American Muslims 89

CHAPTER SIX
The European Pillar of the Network 91
Contending Visions of Islam in Europe 92
Selecting Appropriate Partners 95
Moderate European Muslim Organizations 98

CHAPTER SEVEN
The Southeast Asian Pillar of the Network 105
Moderate Religious Educational Institutions 106
    Islamic Schools (*Pesantren* and *Madrasas*) 106
    Islamic Universities 108
Media 110
Democracy-Building Institutions 110
Regional Network-Building Efforts 111

CHAPTER EIGHT
The Middle East Component 113
Democracy-Building Projects 116
Regional Network-Building Efforts 117
Democracy Building in Iraq 117

CHAPTER NINE
**Secular Muslims: A Forgotten Dimension in the
    War of Ideas** 121
Secular Muslim Organizations 128
    Institutions Solely Devoted to the Promotion of a
        Secular Islam 129
    Rationalist/Humanist Organizations That Support
        Muslim Secularism 130
Online Platforms 131
Notable Muslim Secularist Figures and Their Views 133
Manifestos and Position Papers 136

CHAPTER TEN
Conclusions and Recommendations 139
Applying the Lessons of the Cold War 139
Strategic and Institutional Steps... 141
Launching the Initiative... 144

APPENDIXES
A. U.S. Foreign Assistance Framework 147
B. Documents 149

References 171

Figure and Tables

Figure

A.1.   U.S. Foreign Assistance Framework as of
October 12, 2006 147

Tables

S.1.   Networking Challenges: The Cold War
and the Middle East Today.. xvi
3.1.   Networking Challenges: The Cold War
and the Middle East Today..37

Summary

Radical and dogmatic interpretations of Islam have gained ground in recent years in many Muslim societies. While there are many reasons for this, and while a large and growing body of literature continues to be engaged in exploring them, it is clear that structural factors play a large part. The prevalence of authoritarian political structures and the atrophy of civil-society institutions throughout much of the Muslim world have left the mosque as one of the few avenues for the expression of popular dissatisfaction with prevailing political, economic, and social conditions. In the case of some authoritarian states, radical Muslims present themselves as the only viable alternative to the status quo. They wage their battles in the mass media and political arena of their respective countries—either overtly or underground, depending on the degree of political repression.

By and large, radicals (as well as authoritarian governments) have been successful in intimidating, marginalizing, or silencing moderate Muslims—those who share the key dimensions of democratic culture—to varying degrees.[1] Sometimes, as has happened in Egypt, Iran, and Sudan, liberal Muslim intellectuals are murdered or forced to flee overseas. Even in relatively liberal Indonesia, radicals have resorted to

---

[1]   Those dimensions include support for democracy and internationally recognized human rights, including gender equality and freedom of worship, respect for diversity, acceptance of nonsectarian sources of law, and opposition to terrorism and illegitimate forms of violence. This is further discussed in Chapter Five, "Road Map for Moderate Network Building in the Muslim World."

violence and threats of violence to intimidate opponents. Increasingly, these tactics are being employed in the Muslim diaspora in the West.

Aside from a willingness to resort to violence to compel fellow Muslims to conform to their religious and political views, radicals enjoy two critical advantages over moderate and liberal Muslims. The first is money. Saudi funding for the export of the Wahhabi version of Islam over the last three decades has had the effect, whether intended or not, of promoting the growth of religious extremism throughout the Muslim world. The radicals' second advantage is organization. Radical groups have developed extensive networks over the years, which are themselves embedded in a dense net of international relationships.

This asymmetry in resources and organization explains why radicals, a small minority in almost all Muslim countries, have influence disproportionate to their numbers. As liberal and moderate Muslims generally do not have the organizational tools to effectively counter the radicals, the creation of moderate Muslim networks would provide moderates with a platform to amplify their message, as well as some protection from extremists. It would also provide them a measure of protection from their own governments, which sometimes repress moderates because they provide a more acceptable alternative to authoritarian rule than do the extremists.

Since moderates lack the resources to create these networks themselves, their creation may require an external catalyst. Some argue that the United States, as a majority non-Muslim country, cannot perform this role. Indeed, the obstacles to effectively influencing socio-political developments abroad should not be underestimated. Nevertheless, with considerable experience fostering networks of people committed to free and democratic ideas dating back to the Cold War, the United States has a critical role to play in leveling the playing field for moderates.

In this report we describe, first, how network building was actually done during the Cold War—how the United States identified and supported partners and how it attempted to avoid endangering them. Second, we analyze the similarities and the differences between the Cold War environment and today's struggle with radical Islamism and how these similarities and differences affect U.S. efforts to build networks today. Third, we examine current U.S. strategies and programs of engagement with the Muslim world. Finally, informed by the efforts of the Cold War and previous RAND work on the ideological tendencies in the Muslim world, we develop a "road map" for the construction of moderate Muslim networks and institutions. A key finding of this report—which one of our reviewers notes is particularly important—is that the U.S. government and its allies need, but thus far have failed, to develop clear criteria for partnerships with authentic moderates. The net result, already visible, is the discouragement of truly moderate Muslims.[2]

The Lessons of the Cold War

The efforts of the United States and its partners during the early years of the Cold War to help build free and democratic institutions and organizations hold lessons for the current Global War on Terrorism. At the onset of the Cold War, the Soviet Union could count on the allegiance not only of strong Communist parties in Western Europe (some of which were the largest and best-organized parties in their respective countries and appeared to be poised on the verge of coming to power through democratic means) but also of a plethora of organizations—labor unions, youth and student organizations, and journalists' associations—that gave Soviet-backed elements effective control of important sectors of society. Outside Western Europe, Soviet allies included a number of "liberation movements" struggling against colonial rule. Therefore, the success of U.S. containment policy required (in addition to the military shield provided by U.S. nuclear and conventional forces) the creation of parallel democratic institutions to contest Communist domination of civil society. The close link between the U.S. grand strategy and its efforts to build democratic networks was a key ingredient in the overall success of the U.S. policy of containment; as such, it provides a model for policymakers today.

One important feature of U.S. and allied Cold War network-building initiatives was the link between the public and private sectors.

---

[2]   Hilled Fradkin, review of report, October 2006.

Within the United States and Europe, there was already an intellectual movement against Communism, particularly among the non-Communist left. What was needed was money and organization to turn individual efforts into a coherent campaign. The United States did not create these networks out of thin air; they were born of wider cultural and political movements that the United States and other governments quietly fostered.

In almost all of these endeavors the U.S. government acted like a foundation. It evaluated projects to determine whether they promoted U.S. objectives, provided funding for them, and then adopted a hands-off approach, allowing the organizations it supported to fulfill their objectives without interference. Like any foundation, the U.S. government set out guidelines on how its money was to be spent. However, U.S. officials generally realized that the greater the distance between their government and the sponsored organization, the more likely the organization's activities would succeed.

Today, the United States faces a number of challenges in constructing democratic networks in the Muslim world that mirror those faced by policymakers at the beginning of the Cold War. Three particular challenges seem especially relevant. First, in the late 1940s and early 1950s, U.S. policymakers debated whether their network-building efforts should be offensive or defensive. Some believed the United States should pursue an offensive strategy that sought to destroy Communist rule in Eastern Europe and the Soviet Union by aiding, overtly and covertly, groups inside those countries that were actively engaged in attempts to overthrow Communist governments. Others believed in a more defensive strategy focused on "containing" the Soviet threat by bolstering democratic forces in Western Europe, Asia, and Latin America. Although for the most part, the defensive strategy prevailed, the United States also sought to reverse the flow of ideas: instead of Communist ideas flowing into the West via the Soviet Union and its front organizations, democratic ideas could infiltrate behind the Iron Curtain via newly established information networks.

A second challenge policymakers in the Cold War faced was maintaining the credibility of the groups that the United States was supporting. The organizers of U.S. network-building efforts tried to minimize the risks to these groups by, first, maintaining some distance between these organizations and the U.S. government, and, second, by selecting prominent individuals with a great deal of personal credibility for leadership positions in the networks. The U.S. government also supported the network-building activities of independent organizations such as the American Federation of Labor.

A third key challenge confronting U.S. policymakers was deciding just how broad the anti-Communist coalition should be. For instance, should it include Socialists who had turned against Communism but nevertheless were critical of many aspects of U.S. policy? In the end, the United States decided that anyone could be part of the coalition as long as certain basic principles were subscribed to. For example, the membership ticket to the Congress of Cultural Freedom was agreement to an anti-totalitarian consensus. Disagreement with U.S. policy was allowed—and even encouraged—because it helped to establish the credibility and independence of supported organizations.

Similarities and Differences Between the Cold War Environment and the Muslim World Today

Three broad parallels stand out between the Cold War environment and today. First, the United States, both in the late 1940s and today, was and is confronting a new and confusing geopolitical environment with new security threats. At the beginning of the Cold War the threat was a global Communist movement led by a nuclear-armed Soviet Union; today it is a global jihadist movement striking against the West with acts of mass-casualty terrorism. Second, as was the case in the 1940s, we have witnessed the creation of large, new U.S.-government bureaucracies to combat these threats. Finally, and most importantly, during the early Cold War years there was widespread recognition that the United States and its allies were engaged in an ideological conflict. Policymakers understood this conflict would be contested in and across diplomatic, economic, military, and psychological dimensions. Today, as recognized by the Defense Department in its *Quadrennial Defense Review Report*, the United States is involved in a war that is "both a battle of arms and a battle of ideas," in which ultimate victory can only be won "when extremist ideologies are discredited in the eyes of their host populations and tacit supporters."[3]

Of course, as with all historical analogies it is important to note the differences as well as the similarities between the past and the present. As a nation-state, the Soviet Union had state interests to protect, defined geographical borders, and a clear government structure. Today, by contrast, the United States confronts shadowy nonstate actors that control no territory (although some have been able to establish sanctuaries outside of state control), reject the norms of the international system, and are not subject to normal means of deterrence. Table S.1 summarizes the key differences between the Cold War environment and the environment in the Muslim world today.

Table S.1
Networking Challenges: The Cold War and the Middle East Today

	Cold War	Middle East (Today)
Role of civil society	Historically strong	Historically not strong but developing
Hostility between United States and targeted society/ government	Open hostility between Soviet Union and United States Western societies favorable United States seen as liberator in Western Europe	U.S. democracy promotion and moderate network building is seen by authoritarian U.S. Middle East security partners as destabilizing United States not seen as liberator
Intellectual and historical ties	Strong	Weak
Adversary's ideology	Secular	Religion based
Nature of opposing networks	Centrally controlled	Loose or no central control
Policy challenges	Less complex	More complex

---

[3] U.S. Department of Defense, *Quadrennial Defense Review Report*, February 6, 2006, pp. 21–22.

U.S. Programs of Engagement with the Muslim World

In the wake of the 9/11 terrorist attacks, a great deal of resources and attention were devoted to the physical security of American citizens and territory. At the same time, with the recognition that combating terrorism was not only a matter of bringing terrorists to justice and diminishing their capacity to operate, there was an effort to understand and address the "root causes" of terrorism. The National Security Strategy document of September 2002 elucidated a refined conception of security that emphasizes the consequences of internal conditions of other states—particularly the lack of democracy. This theme was to be reinforced over the course of the next several years, from the 9/11 Commission Report to, perhaps most dramatically, President Bush's second inaugural address.

From its prominence in a series of high-profile documents and speeches, the President's "Freedom Agenda" can be considered a U.S. "grand strategy" in the Global War on Terrorism. However, a consensus on how to identify and support partners in the "war of ideas" has not yet emerged. Specifically, there is currently no explicit U.S. policy to help build moderate Muslim networks, although such network-building activity is taking place as a by-product of other U.S. assistance programs. At the heart of the approach we propose is making the building of moderate Muslim networks an explicit goal of U.S. government programs.

Moderate network building can proceed at three levels: (1) bolstering existing networks; (2) identifying potential networks and promoting their inception and growth; and (3) contributing to the underlying conditions of pluralism and tolerance that are favorable to the growth of these networks. Although there are a number of U.S. government programs that have effects on the first two levels, most U.S. efforts to date fall within the third level, due partly to organizational preferences and to the fact that in many parts of the Muslim world there are few existing moderate networks or organizations with which the United States could partner. In addition, when promoting the formation of moderate networks, the United States must contend with both repressive socio-political environments and high levels of anti-Americanism throughout much of the Muslim world.

For the most part, most efforts of the U.S. government that concern us fall into the categories of democracy promotion, civil-society development, and public diplomacy.

Democracy Promotion

Through traditional diplomacy, the United States engages in state-to-state dialogue and has crafted incentives such as The Millennium Challenge Account for states to join the "community of democracies." Publicly and privately, the United States emphasizes the benefits of adopting liberal democratic values of equity, tolerance, pluralism, the rule of law, and respect for civil and human rights. This emphasis on democratic values serves to contribute to the development of a political and social environment that facilitates the formation of moderate networks.

In addition, both the Department of State and the U.S. Agency for International Development (USAID) have specific democracy-promotion mandates. To translate these policy goals into action, the Department of State and USAID contract with nongovernmental organizations (NGOs), principally the National Endowment for Democracy (NED), the International Republican Institute (IRI), the National Democratic Institute (NDI), the Asia Foundation, and the Center for the Study of Islam and Democracy (CSID). These are all nonprofit organizations funded by the U.S. government.

Although it is far from the largest U.S. program of engagement with the Muslim world, the Middle East Partnership Initiative (MEPI) represents a high-profile attempt to break free from pre-9/11 standard approaches. MEPI structures its programs on four thematic "pillars"— political reform, economic reform, education, and women's empowerment—and directly supports indigenous NGOs on a more innovative and flexible basis. As a new office in the Department of State's Bureau of Near Eastern Affairs (NEA), MEPI was designed to veer away from the conventional government-to-government approach by relying on U.S. NGOs, as implementing contractors, to disburse small grants directly to indigenous NGOs within the framework of the four "pillars."

In 2004, the United States, together with partners in the group of eight heads of state of major economic powers (G8), attempted to inject a multilateral approach with the launching of the Broader Middle East and North Africa Initiative (BMENA). In the summer of 2006 BMENA launched an effort to replicate the model of the Asia Foundation—the most successful NGO in promoting programs to develop civil-society institutions—and tailor it to the Middle East region.

Civil-Society Development

The promotion of democracy goes hand in hand with the development of civil society; in fact, many in academia and the policy world consider civil society a necessary precursor to democracy. Civil society refers broadly to a set of institutions and values that serves both as a buffer and a critical link between the state and individuals, families, and clans; it is manifested when voluntary civic and social organizations (such as NGOs) can stand in opposition to forces brought by the state. While civil society develops most easily in democracies, its development is both possible and desirable in non- and pre-democratic states.

The development of civil society and network building are integrally linked: both mutually reinforcing and mutually dependent. In theory, as civil society emerges, moderate networks follow, and vice versa. In practice, U.S. efforts at civil-society development are broader than democracy promotion—they include all of the programs designed to promote democracy plus those with mandates not squarely involved with democracy per se. These include programs promoting economic opportunity, independent and responsible media, environmental protection minority or gender rights, and access to health care and education. This broad approach takes a long view, gradually building democracy and liberal values through a grassroots, bottom-up effort. Such a strategy presents specific challenges to standard operating procedures of the U.S. government, particularly the Department of State, which traditionally has focused on engaging with governments.

Both democracy promotion and civil-society building face two primary obstacles: active resistance by authoritarian regimes and a lack of tangible performance measurement criteria. Government resistance manifests itself in laws prohibiting NGO formation or acceptance of external support, strict monitoring of NGO activity and, more recently, expulsion of officials (Bahrain) and suspension of activities (Egypt).

On the public diplomacy front, Secretary of State Condoleezza Rice has engaged in an effort to have the Department of State and the U.S. government at large pursue "transformational diplomacy," in which U.S. government officials inculcate public diplomacy into both policy design and implementation. But within the government, the objectives of public diplomacy remain varied. Not surprisingly, its effects are the most diffuse and hardest to measure.

The dominant mechanisms to deliver public diplomacy to the Muslim world have been radio and satellite television broadcasting, primarily Radio Sawa and the U.S. Middle East Television Network (Al Hurra). While Al Hurra has been heavily criticized for its inability to gain market share, Radio Sawa has been fairly successful in building an audience. Success in building an audience, however, does not clearly translate to net gains in general moderation or more tangible forms of moderate institution building. It is far from clear that, despite their high cost ($700 million a year, or ten times the amount allocated to MEPI), either Radio Sawa or Al Hurra has been able to positively shape attitudes in the Muslim world toward U.S. policies.

Road Map to Moderate Network Building

After reviewing the strategies that were most effective in building a strong and credible body of alternate values, influential dissidents, and reliable counterparts during the Cold War, we surveyed the Muslim world's intellectual, organizational, and ideational makeup. In parallel, we evaluated the U.S. government's current public diplomacy effort to reshape political discourse in the Middle East. From this research, we developed the implementation path described below.

The first step is for the U.S. government and its allies to make a clear decision to build moderate networks and to create an explicit link between this goal and overall U.S. strategy and programs. Effective implementation of this strategy requires the creation of an institutional structure within the U.S. government to guide, support, oversee, and continuously monitor the effort. Within the framework of this structure, the U.S. government must build up the necessary expertise and capacity to execute the strategy, which includes

1. An ever-evolving and ever-sharpening set of criteria that distinguishes true moderates from opportunists and from extremists camouflaged as moderates, and liberal secularists from authoritarian secularists. The U.S. government needs to have the ability to make situational decisions to *knowingly* and for tactical reasons support individuals outside of that range under specific circumstances.
2. An international database of partners (individuals, groups, organizations, institutions, parties, etc.)
3. Mechanisms for monitoring, refining, and overseeing programs, projects, and decisions. These should include a feedback loop to allow for inputs and corrections from those partners who have been found to be most trustworthy.

The network-building effort could initially focus on a core group of reliable partners whose ideological orientation is known, and work outward from there (i.e., following the methodology of underground organizations). Once the ideology of any newly targeted organizations has been firmly ascertained, the United States could begin to increase levels of local autonomy.

Our approach calls for fundamental changes to the current, symmetric strategy of engagement with the Muslim world. The current approach identifies the problem area as the Middle East and structures its programs accordingly. That area is much too large, too diverse, too opaque, and too much in the grip of non-moderate sectors to allow for much traction (as reflected in the experience of MEPI). It can absorb very large amounts of resources with little or no impact. Instead, the United States should pursue a new policy that is *asymmetric* and *selective*. As in the Cold War, U.S. efforts should avoid the opponent's center of gravity and instead concentrate on the partners, programs, and regions where U.S. support has the greatest likelihood of impacting the war of ideas.

With regard to partners, it will be important to identify the social sectors that would constitute the building blocks of the proposed networks. Priority should be given to

1. Liberal and secular Muslim academics and intellectuals
2. Young moderate religious scholars
3. Community activists
4. Women's groups engaged in gender equality campaigns
5. Moderate journalists and writers.

The United States should ensure visibility and platforms for these individuals. For example, U.S. officials should ensure that individuals from these groups are included in congressional visits, making them better known to policymakers and helping to maintain U.S. support and resources for the public diplomacy effort.

Assistance programs should be organized around the sectors listed above, and would include

1. *Democratic education*, particularly programs that use Islamic texts and traditions for authoritative teachings that support democratic and pluralistic values
2. *Media*. Support for moderate media is critical to combating media domination by anti-democratic and conservative Muslim elements.
3. *Gender equality*. The issue of women's rights is a major battleground in the war of ideas within Islam, and women's rights advocates operate in very adverse environments. Promotion of gender equality is a critical component of any project to empower moderate Muslims.
4. *Policy advocacy*. Islamists have political agendas, and moderates need to engage in policy advocacy as well. Advocacy activities are important in order to shape the political and legal environment in the Muslim world.

With regard to geographic focus, we propose a shift of priorities from the Middle East to the regions of the Muslim world where greater freedom of action is possible, the environment is more open to activism and influence, and success is more likely and more perceptible. The current approach is defensive and reactive. Built on the recognition that radical ideas are originating in the Middle East and from there are being disseminated to the rest of the Muslim world, including the Muslim diaspora in Europe and North America, this approach identifies the ideas and efforts of the extremists in the Middle East and seeks to counter them. Seeking to reverse this flow of ideas represents a much better policy. Important texts originating from thinkers, intellectuals, activists, and leaders in the Muslim diaspora, in Turkey, in Indonesia, and elsewhere should be translated into Arabic and disseminated widely. This does not mean that core areas should be abandoned. Rather, the goal should be to hold the ground in expectation of opportunities for advancement, which can arise at any moment.

There is some "networking" of moderates currently going on, but it is random and insufficiently considered. Networking individuals and groups whose credentials as moderates have not been firmly established or networking pseudo-moderates not only is a waste of resources, it can be counterproductive. The Danish imams who caused the cartoon controversy to spiral into an international conflagration had earlier been presumed to be moderates and had been the beneficiaries of state support, including travel and networking opportunities. Closer scrutiny after the incident revealed that these individuals were not true moderates at all.

Public diplomacy currently lags behind the media curve and needs to pay closer attention to contemporary circumstances. Radio was an important medium during the Cold War, helping isolated populations gain better access to information. Today, citizens of the Muslim world are overwhelmed by a vast amount of often inaccurate and biased information, and content and delivery stand in a much more demanding relationship to each other. Radio Sawa and Al Hurra are perceived as proxies for the U.S. government and, despite their high cost, have not resulted in positively shaping attitudes toward the United States. We believe that the funds spent on Radio Sawa and Al Hurra television would be better spent supporting local media outlets and journalists that adhere to a democratic and pluralistic agenda.

We propose to launch the initiative recommended in this report with a workshop, to be held in Washington or another appropriate venue, gathering a small, representative group of Muslim moderates. This workshop would serve to obtain their input and their support for the initiative and to prepare the agenda and list of participants for an international conference modeled on the Congress of Cultural Freedom.

If this event were successful, we would then work with the core group to hold an international conference to be held in a venue of symbolic significance for Muslims, for instance, Córdoba in Spain, to launch a standing organization to combat radical Islamism.

Acknowledgments

The authors wish to thank all those who made this study possible. First of all, we wish to thank the Smith Richardson Foundation for providing the funding that made this publication possible and in particular our project officer, Allan Song, who provided invaluable input in the conceptual stage of this project.

We have many to thank among academics and research institutions, government officials, members of nongovernmental organizations, and civil-society activists who cooperated with us in our research. We are greatly in the debt of our reviewers, Hillel Fradkin, Director, Center on Islam, Democracy and the Future of the Muslim World, The Hudson Institute; and Dalia Dassa Kaye, The RAND Corporation. In the academic and policy community we particularly wish to thank Husain Haqqani and Eric Brown of The Hudson Institute; Ambassadors Dennis Ross and Robert Satloff of The Washington Institute for Near East Policy; the staff of the U.S. Commission on International Religious Freedom, particularly Joseph Crapa, Tad Stahnke, Dwight Bashir, and Scott Flipse; Paul Marshall of Freedom House; Abdeslam Maghraoui and Mona Yacoubian of the United States Institute of Peace; Daniel Pipes; Stephen Schwartz for his valuable insights on Sufism; Adam Garfinkle; Radwan Masmoudi of the Center for the Study of Islam and Democracy; Michael Whine, Defence and Group Relations Director of the Board of Deputies of British Jews; and Italian researcher Valentina Colombo.

We would also like to acknowledge Ross Johnson for his insights into Radio Liberty's relationship with the Central Intelligence Agency and former Radio Liberty staff member Gene Sosin for his reflections on early Radio Liberty operations. For assisting with our assessment of U.S. government programs of engagement with the Muslim world, we thank Deputy Assistant Secretary of State for Near Eastern Affairs J. Scott Carpenter; Alberto Fernandez, Bureau of Near Eastern Affairs, Department of State; as well as a number of current U.S. government officials serving within the United States Agency for International Development and the Department of State, and members of congressional staff. We also thank Steven Cook, Council on Foreign Relations; John Esposito, Georgetown University; Juliette Kayyem, Harvard University; Ambassador Daniel Kurtzer, Princeton University; Joseph Nye, Harvard University; and Gary Sick, Columbia University.

Those in the Muslim world who assisted the research for this project and earlier RAND research on trends within Islam are too numerous to list here. However, we would particularly like to thank the following: in Indonesia, former Muhammadiyah Chairman Ahmad Syafii Maarif; Muhammadiyah Youth Central Board Chairman Abdul Mu'ti; State Islamic University Rector Azyumardi Azra; former Liberal Muslim Network head Ulil Abshar-Abdalla; M. Syafi'i Anwar, Executive Director of the International Center for Islam and Pluralism; Jusuf Wanandi and Rizal Sukma of Jakarta's Centre for Strategic and International Studies; in the Philippines, Carolina Hernandez, President of the Institute for Strategic and Development Studies; Amina Rasul-Bernardo of the Philippine Council for Islam and Democracy; Carmen Abubakar of the Institute of Islamic Studies of the University of the Philippines; and Taha Basman of the Philippine Islamic Council; in Singapore, Ambassador-at-Large Tommy Koh; Islam analyst Sue-Ann Lee; Suzaina Kadir; and many others. We also thank former Malaysian Deputy Prime Minister Anwar Ibrahim, currently at Georgetown University.

We also wish to thank Mansur Escudero, Co-Secretary General of the Islamic Commission of Spain; Yusuf Fernandez, Secretary, Muslim Federation of Spain (FEME); Shamlan Al-Essa, Director, Center for Strategic and Future Studies, Kuwait University; Ahmed Bishara, Secretary-General, Kuwait National Democratic Movement; Mohammed Al-Jassem, editor-in-chief of Kuwait's *Al-Watan* newspaper; Shafeeq

Ghabra, President of the American University of Kuwait; Mohamed Al Roken, Assistant Dean of the Faculty of Sharia Law at the UAE University at Al Ain; and Abdulla Latif Al Shamsi.

Within RAND, we thank David Aaron, Director, Center for Middle East Public Policy (CMEPP), and Susan Everingham, Director of International Programs, under whose guidance this research was done; our research assistant Kristen Cordell, for her invaluable assistance in putting together this project; and our administrative assistant, Rosa Maria Torres. Finally we would like to thank the staff of RAND Publications, in particular Stephan Kistler, our editor; Lynn Rubenfeld, our production editor; Eileen La Russo, who designed the cover; and John Warren, marketing director.

Abbreviations

AFL	American Federation of Labor
Amcomlib	American Committee for Liberation from Bolshevism
BBG	Broadcasting Board of Governors
BMENA	Broader Middle East and North Africa
CFCM	*Conseil Française du Culte Musluman* [French Council of the Muslim Religion]
CIA	Central Intelligence Agency
CIO	Congress of Industrial Organizations
CMEPP	Center for Middle East Public Policy (RAND)
Cominform	Communist Information Bureau
CSID	Center for the Study of Islam and Democracy
DRL	Bureau of Democracy, Human Rights, and Labor (U.S. State Department)
FEC	Free Europe Committee
FEERI	*Federación Española de Entidades Religiosas Islámicas* [Spanish Federation of Islamic Religious Entities]
FNMF	*Fédération Nationale des Musulmans de France* [National Federation of Muslims of France]

FTUC	Free Trade Union Committee
GAO	Government Acountability Office
HAMAS	*Harakat al-Muqawama al-Islamiyya* [Islamic Resistance Movement] (Palestinian Territories)
IAIN	*Institut Agama Islam Negeri* [State Institute for Islamic Studies] (Indonesia)
ICFTU	International Congress of Free Trade Unions
ICIP	International Center for Islam and Pluralism
IOD	International Organization Division (CIA)
IRD	Information Research Department (British Foreign Office)
IRI	International Republican Institute
ISC	International Student Conference
IUS	International Union of Students
MCB	Muslim Council of Britain
MEPI	Middle East Partnership Initiative
NCFE	National Committee for a Free Europe
NDI	National Democratic Institute
NEA	Bureau of Near Eastern Affairs (U.S. State Department)
NED	National Endowment for Democracy
NGO	Nongovernmental organization
NSA	National Student Association
NSC	National Security Council
NSRD	National Security Research Division (RAND)

OECD	Organisation for Economic Co-Operation and Development
OPC	Office of Policy Coordination
PAS	*Parti Islam SeMalaysia* [Islamic Party of Malaysia]
PCID	Philippine Council for Islam and Democracy
PJD	*Parti de Justice et Développement* [Party of Justice and Development] (Morocco)
RFE	Radio Free Europe
RL	Radio Liberty
RRU	Rapid Reaction Unit (U.S. State Department Bureau of Public Affairs)
UAE	United Arab Emirates
UCIDE	*Unión de Comunidades Islámicas de España* [Union of Islamic Communities of Spain]
UNDP	United Nations Development Programme
USAID	U.S. Agency for International Development
USIA	U.S. Information Agency
USINDO	The United States–Indonesia Society
WFDY	World Federation of Democratic Youth
WFTU	World Federation of Trade Unions
WML	*Rabitat al-'Alam al-Islami* [World Muslim League]

CHAPTER ONE

Introduction

The Challenge of Radical Islam

Radical and dogmatic interpretations of Islam have gained ground in recent years in many Muslim societies. While there are many reasons for this, and while a large and growing body of literature continues to be engaged in exploring them, a case can be made that structural reasons play a large part. The prevalence of authoritarian political structures in Muslim, and especially Arab, societies and the atrophy of civil-society institutions throughout much of the Muslim world have left the mosque as one of the few avenues for the expression of popular dissatisfaction with prevailing political, economic, and social conditions. In the case of some authoritarian states, radical Muslims present themselves as the only viable alternative to the status quo. They wage their battles in the mass media and the political arena of their respective countries—either overtly or underground, depending on the degree of political repression.

By and large, radicals have been successful in intimidating, marginalizing, or silencing moderate Muslims—those who share the key dimensions of democratic culture—to varying degrees.[1] Sometimes, as has happened in Egypt, Iran, and Sudan, liberal Muslim intellec-

---

[1] Those dimensions include support for democracy and internationally recognized human rights, including gender equality and freedom of worship, respect for diversity, acceptance of nonsectarian sources of law, and opposition to terrorism and illegitimate forms of violence. This is further discussed in Chapter Five, "Road Map for Moderate Network Building in the Muslim World."

tuals are murdered or forced to flee overseas. Even in relatively liberal Indonesia, radicals have resorted to violence and threats of violence to intimidate opponents. Radical clerics there issued a fatwa authorizing the killing of a liberal opponent for apostasy, and members of radical groups attacked the premises and homes of members of the heterodox Ahmadiyah sect and disrupted a public lecture by former President Abdurrahman Wahid. Increasingly, these tactics are being employed in the Muslim diaspora in the West, particularly in Europe, where prominent liberal and secular Muslims have received death threats.[2]

Aside from a willingness to resort to violence to compel fellow Muslims to conform to their religious and political views, radicals enjoy two critical advantages over moderate and liberal Muslims. The first is money. Saudi funding for the export of the Wahhabi version of Islam over the last three decades has had the effect, whether intended or not, of promoting the growth of religious extremism throughout the Muslim world. The Saudi-based Al-Haramain Foundation was closed because its branches were funding terrorist organizations from Bosnia to Southeast Asia.

The radicals' second advantage is organization. Radical groups have developed extensive networks over the years, which are themselves embedded in a dense net of international relationships. Some of these international networks were organized under official Saudi auspices. The *Rabitat al-'Alam al-Islami* [World Muslim League] (WML) was established in 1962 with the chief mufti of Saudi Arabia as its president. The WML was intended to project the Saudi version of Islam into the international arena. It also brought about a closer association between Wahhabis and other Salafis. The Wahhabi international network also includes the International Islamic Federation of Student Organizations, the World Assembly of Muslim Youth, and the Muslim Student Association of North America and Canada.

This asymmetry in organization and resources explains why radicals, a small minority in almost all Muslim countries, have influence disproportionate to their numbers. The imbalance between the means

---

2 "Moderate Danish Muslims Targets of Attacks and Death Threats," text of report by Danish *Politiken* Web site, BBC Worldwide Monitoring, November 22, 2004.

of radicals and moderates could also have significant consequences for the "war of ideas" underway throughout the Muslim world. The United States and other Western countries can do little to affect the outcome of this "war of ideas" directly, as only Muslims themselves have the credibility to challenge the misuse of Islam by extremists. However, moderates will not be able to successfully challenge radicals until the playing field is leveled, which the West can help accomplish by promoting the creation of moderate Muslim networks.

Potential Partners and Allies

The potential partners of the West in the struggle against radical Islamism are moderate, liberal, and secular Muslims with political values congruent to the universal values underlying all modern liberal societies. We refer to "liberal" and "moderate" Muslims not as a means of classification, but rather as shorthand for those groups that eschew violent and intolerant ideologies and that, therefore, are potential partners for the United States and its friends and allies in the ideological struggle against radical Islamism. Distinguishing between authentic moderates and extremists masquerading as moderates presents a major difficulty in Western programs of engagement with Muslim communities. A key finding of this report—which one of our reviewers notes is particularly important—is that the U.S. government and its allies need, but thus far have failed, to develop clear criteria identifying authentic moderates.[3] The net result, already visible, is the discouragement of truly moderate Muslims. We hope that one of the major contributions of this report will be the establishment of a set of criteria for identifying moderates. These criteria are laid out in Chapter Five of the report, "Road Map for Democratic Network Building in the Muslim World."[4]

---

[3] Hilled Fradkin, review of report, October 2006.

[4] There are some who oppose the use of the term "moderate" Muslims and prefer "main-stream" Muslims, on the grounds that the United States has no standing to determine who are good Muslims and who are not. However, the same problem arises in defining who

In an important article in *The Wall Street Journal* on December 30, 2005, former Indonesian president and world-renowned religious statesman Abdurrahman Wahid listed sixteen strengths of moderates in confronting religious extremism, but pointed out that though potentially decisive, most of these advantages remain latent or diffuse and require mobilization to be effective in confronting fundamentalist ideology.[5] Liberal and moderate Muslims generally do not have the organizational tools to effectively counter the radicals. Most liberal Muslims acknowledge that there is no liberal Muslim movement, only individuals who are often isolated and beleaguered. In the view of many moderate Muslims, the creation of moderate and liberal networks is essential to retrieve Islam from the radicals. The antidote to radicalism is the very same organizational methods used by the radicals themselves—network-building and effective communications—to disseminate enlightened and moderate interpretations of Islam.

The central problem is that moderates lack the financial and organizational resources to create these networks themselves; the initial impulse for their creation may require an external catalyst. While the United States has a critical role to play in leveling the playing field for moderates, there are, of course, obstacles. In many parts of the Muslim world there are few existing moderate networks or organizations with which the United States could partner. Some also argue that the United States, as a majority non-Muslim country, does not have the credibility to successfully foment moderate Muslim networks. Indeed, the obstacles to effectively influencing socio-political developments abroad should not be underestimated. Nevertheless, the United States has considerable experience fostering networks of people committed to free and democratic ideas dating back to the Cold War. What is needed at this stage is to derive lessons from the experience of the Cold War, determine their applicability to the conditions of the Muslim

---

belongs to the "mainstream" and who does not; moreover, there may be circumstances where the mainstream is not moderate.

5   Abdurrahman Wahid, "Right Islam vs. Wrong Islam," *The Wall Street Journal*, December 30, 2005. The text of the article is reproduced in Appendix B.

world today, and develop a "road map" for the construction of moderate Muslim networks and coalitions.

Scholars, such as Robert Satloff in his book *The Battle of Ideas in the War on Terror*, have made useful suggestions on how to "extend a helping hand" to American allies in the struggle against radical Islam.[6] We also are not the first people to suggest looking at the U.S. Cold War program as a model for building networks. William Rugh, in his essay "Fixing Public Diplomacy for Arab and Muslim Audiences," recounts some of the public diplomacy tools the U.S. Information Agency (USIA) used during the Cold War and discusses how these techniques could be utilized today.[7] Derk Kinnane suggests, as we do, that the proper course is building an international platform for anti-Islamist Muslims similar to the anti-Communist organizations organized in Western Europe during the Cold War.[8] However, other authors take issue with an emphasis on the importance of civil-society development in ending the Cold War.[9]

---

[6]   Robert Satloff, *The Battle of Ideas in the War on Terror*, Washington, D.C.: Washington Institute for Near East Policy, 2004, pp. 60–69. Satloff makes three broad suggestions. First, that the United States identify and support potential allies which could be organized under a collective umbrella of opposition to Islamist ideas. Second, that the United States empower its partners in their battle against the rising tide of Islamist nongovernmental organizations (NGOs). Islamist NGOs, under the guise of providing social services to local communities, have become a major pathway for spreading Islamist thought and terrorism throughout the Muslim world. Third, provide educational opportunities for Muslim youth, with a particular emphasis on English. A working knowledge of English provides a window on the world to Muslim youth, allowing them to access global instead of just local information resources.

[7]   William Rugh, "Fixing Public Diplomacy for Arab and Muslim Audiences," in Adam Garfinkle, ed., *A Practical Guide to Winning the War on Terrorism*, Stanford, Calif.: Hoover Institution Press, 2004, pp. 145–162.

[8]   Derk Kinnane, "Winning Over the Muslim Mind," *The National Interest*, Spring 2004, pp. 93–99.

[9]   Jeffrey Kopstein, for instance, states that "From western Europe's perspective, democracy promotion after 1989 was primarily a top-down effort. The true *dramatis personae* of history in their reading of 1989 were found in the Kremlin and not in the streets of Warsaw or Budapest. Without then-Soviet president Mikhail Gorbachev's determination to end the Cold War, there would have been no opening in the East. Political leaders and diplomats, not demonstrators, brought about regime change." Jeffrey Kopstein, "The Transatlantic

In this report, we describe how network building was actually done during the Cold War—how the United States identified and supported partners and how it attempted to avoid endangering its partners; we then analyze the similarities and the differences between the Cold War environment and today's struggle with radical Islamism. After examining current U.S. strategies and programs of engagement with the Muslim world, we develop a road map for building moderate Muslim networks and institutions in different regions of the Muslim world.

Divide over Democracy Promotion," *The Washington Quarterly*, Vol. 29, No. 2, Spring 2006, p. 87.

CHAPTER TWO

The Cold War Experience

The propaganda and cultural-infiltration efforts of the United States and Britain during the early years of the Cold War hold valuable lessons for the Global War on Terrorism. At the onset of the Cold War, the Soviet Union could count on the allegiance not only of strong Communist parties in Western Europe (some of which were the largest and best-organized parties in their respective countries and appeared to be poised on the verge of coming to power through democratic means) but also of a plethora of organizations—labor unions, youth and student organizations, and journalists' associations—that gave Soviet-backed elements effective control of important sectors of society. Outside Western Europe, Soviet allies included a number of "liberation movements" struggling against colonial rule. Therefore, the success of U.S. containment policy required (in addition to the military shield provided by U.S. nuclear and conventional forces) the creation of parallel democratic institutions to contest Communist domination of civil society.

U.S. Grand Strategy at the Beginning of the Cold War

U.S. political warfare efforts against the Soviet Union began at approximately the same time as the grand strategy of containment was put in place. This was no accident. George Kennan, Director of Policy Planning in the Department of State and author of the "long telegram" (which laid out the strategy of containment), and other policymakers saw political warfare as one piece of a broader strategy to reduce Moscow's power and influence. It is essential to briefly review U.S. grand strategy at the beginning of the Cold War in order to fully understand the strategy and thinking behind U.S. network-building activities.

On March 12, 1947, Harry Truman came before a joint session of Congress to announce what became known as the Truman Doctrine. The basic reasoning behind his speech was straightforward. Greece and Turkey had been under Communist pressure to establish governments more friendly to the Soviet Union. The Greek and Turkish governments had been able to resist this pressure up to that point with economic and military assistance from Great Britain, but because of an economic crisis at home Britain was being forced to withdraw this aid. Truman's speech indicated his intention for the United States to supply Greece and Turkey with the arms, economic aid, and military advice that Britain could no longer provide. However, Truman did not stop there, couching his request in terms of a much broader strategy of supporting "free peoples who are resisting attempted subjugation by armed minorities or by outside pressure groups."[1] Kennan was not altogether pleased with Truman's speech, writing that he took exception to it because of the "sweeping nature of the commitments it implied" and that he felt it was "a universal policy rather than one set for a specific set of circumstances."[2] However, this kind of sweeping statement was exactly what President Truman and Assistant Secretary of State Dean Acheson believed was required to motivate Congress and the American people to meet the Communist challenge.

The Truman Doctrine was followed by the Marshall Plan. In a June 5, 1947, commencement address at Harvard University, Secretary of State George C. Marshall announced that America would provide economic recovery funds to European states that were willing to cooperatively plan and implement a unified economic program across Europe. Along with his staff at the Department of State, Kennan provided the strategic rationale for the economic program by arguing that the economic collapse of Europe would make it more likely that the Communists would be able to seize power there. Kennan believed this

---

[1]   David McCullough, *Truman*, New York: Simon and Schuster, 1992, p. 546.

[2]   George Kennan, *Memoirs: 1925–1950*, Boston: Little, Brown, 1967, pp. 319–320.

program should not be directed at combating Communist domination but instead toward restoring the economic health and vigor of European society.[3]

After much debate, the Marshall Plan passed Congress in December 1947 with a $597 million interim aid bill for Austria, France, Italy, and China.[4] Even with the Marshall Plan in place, the year 1948 began bleakly for the United States as twin crises in Italy and France threatened to undermine the entire U.S. Cold War strategy. In an attempt to counteract the Marshall Plan, the Soviet government launched the Communist Information Bureau (Cominform). Of greatest alarm to Western officials was the inclusion of the Communist parties in France and Italy in the Cominform. These parties began to foment rioting and work stoppages to prevent the weak governments in their home countries from joining the Marshall Plan. With elections in both France and Italy scheduled in 1948, a full-fledged test of strength between Communist and non-Communist forces in Western Europe was imminent.

In response to this challenge, the National Security Council (NSC) issued NSC-4, which authorized the Assistant Secretary of State for Public Affairs to formulate and coordinate U.S. information operations.[5] According to NSC-4, the assistant secretary would determine the most effective utilization of all U.S. information facilities and develop interdepartmental plans and programs to influence foreign opinion in a direction favorable to U.S. interests.[6]

These efforts were quickly put to work in an intensive campaign to assist the Christian Democratic party to an election victory over

[3] Wilson Miscamble, *George F. Kennan and the Making of American Foreign Policy 1947–1950*, Princeton, N.J.: Princeton University Press, 1992, p. 50.

[4] Walter L. Hixson, *George F. Kennan: Cold War Iconoclast*, New York: Columbia University Press, 1989, p. 56.

[5] Gregory Mitrovich, *Undermining the Kremlin: America's Strategy to Subvert the Soviet Block, 1947–1956*, Ithaca, N.Y.: Cornell University Press, 2000, p. 17.

[6] Edward P. Lilly, "The Development of American Psychological Operations, 1945–1951," December 19, 1951, Box 22, p. 35, Records of the Psychological Strategy Board, Harry S. Truman Library.

the Communist party in Italy. On the overt side, President Truman broadcast a warning over Voice of America that no economic assistance would be forthcoming if the Communists won the election. The United States also supplied food items, and Italian Americans mounted a letter-writing campaign encouraging their families in Italy to support non-Communist parties. On the covert side, the Central Intelligence Agency (CIA) launched a powerful propaganda effort, supplying newsprint and information to pro-Western newspapers. Among the stories the CIA placed in Italian newspapers were truthful accounts of the brutality of Soviet forces in the Soviet sector of Germany and of the Communist takeovers in Poland, Czechoslovakia, and Hungary.[7] On election day, the Christian Democratic party won a crushing victory, garnering 48.5 percent of the vote. To members of the Truman administration, this victory was a clear demonstration of the utility of propaganda and psychological warfare in defeating political threats abroad.

By late 1948, U.S. grand strategy was embracing containment and "counterforce" (placing pressure on the Soviet Union in a variety of ways in order to curtail Soviet expansive tendencies). This strategy had two pillars: strengthening Western Europe (and later other regions) to discourage Soviet attempts at expansionism and placing pressure on Soviet control over Eastern Europe. The strategy was to be executed through economic (the Marshall Plan), military (NATO and other military alliances), diplomatic, and information activities.

Political Warfare

Kennan outlined his program for political warfare in a May 1948 memo to the NSC.[8] Although it contains some features that go well beyond information and network-building operations, Kennan's program is worth mentioning in order to get a broader perspective of the

---

[7]   Mitrovich, 2000, p. 18.

[8]   Policy Planning Staff to National Security Council, "Organized Political Warfare," 4 May 1948, Record Group 273, Records of the National Security Council, NSC 10/2. National Archives and Records Administration.

role of political warfare in U.S. strategy in the initial stages of the Cold War. Kennan started the paper by providing a definition of political warfare:

> Political warfare is the logical application of Clausewitz's doctrine in time of peace. In the broadest definition, political warfare is the employment of all means at a nation's command, short of war, to achieve its national objectives. Such operations are both overt and covert. They range from such overt activities as political alliances, economic measures, and "white propaganda" to such covert operations as clandestine support of "friendly" foreign elements, "black" psychological warfare and even encouragement of underground resistance in hostile states.[9]

Kennan noted the United States was already engaged in such activities through the Truman Doctrine and the Marshall Plan, which were implemented in response to "aggressive Soviet political warfare" efforts. However, the United States had failed to mobilize all of the resources needed to successfully wage covert political warfare against the Soviet Union.

Kennan's program for political warfare involved four broad categories of activities, some overt and some covert. The first set of "projects" the paper described were plans to set up "liberation committees." These committees were to be "public American organizations" in the traditional American form, "organized public support of resistance to tyranny in foreign countries." Their purpose was threefold: to "act as a foci of national hope" for political refugees from the Soviet bloc, to "provide an inspiration for continuing popular resistance within the countries of the Eastern bloc," and to "serve as a potential nucleus for all-out liberation movements in the event of war."[10] The paper described these efforts as "primarily an overt operation, which, however, should receive covert guidance and possibly assistance from the government." The job of organizing these committees was to be given to "trusted private American citizens" in order to mobilize selected "refugee leaders." These

---

[9]   Policy Planning Staff, 1948.

[10]   Policy Planning Staff, 1948.

refugee leaders were to be given "access to printing and microphones" to keep them alive as public figures in their home countries. This first set of programs was the inspiration for and the organizing principle behind the National Committee for a Free Europe (NCFE) and the American Committee for Liberation from Bolshevism (Amcomlib), the organizations that sponsored Radio Free Europe (RFE) and Radio Liberation (RL), known as Radio Liberty after 1959.

The second set of projects, many of which remain classified, were outright paramilitary actions to undermine Soviet power in Eastern Europe and inside the Soviet Union itself.[11] These were to be undertaken by private American organizations that would establish contact with national underground representatives in free countries, and through these intermediaries pass on assistance and guidance to resistance movements behind the Iron Curtain.[12]

The third set of projects was intended to support indigenous anti-Communist elements in threatened countries of the Free World. France and Italy were specifically cited, as they remained unstable in 1948. This, again, was a covert operation in which "private intermediaries" were to be utilized. Kennan wrote that it was important to "separate" these private organizations from the organizations in the second set of projects, perhaps referring to the front organizations that would funnel arms to groups behind the Iron Curtain.[13] These were the projects most closely linked with network-building activities. Substantial sums were given by the Office of Policy Coordination (OPC) and later the CIA to anti-Communist political parties, labor unions, student groups, and intellectual organizations. How these groups were organized and covertly funded will be discussed in detail in the next section.

The fourth and final projects Kennan mentioned were "preventive direct actions in free countries."[14] These actions were only for "critical necessity" in order to "prevent vital installations, other materials, or

---

[11] Peter Grose, *Operation Rollback: America's Secret War Behind the Iron Curtain*, Boston: Houghton Mifflin, 2000, p. 98.

[12] Grose, 2000, pp. 164–168.

[13] Policy Planning Staff, 1948.

[14] Policy Planning Staff, 1948.

personnel from being (1) sabotaged or liquidated or (2) captured intact by Kremlin agents or agencies."[15] The paper cited examples of these kinds of covert actions such as "control over anti-sabotage activities in the Venezuelan oil fields" and "designation of key individuals threatened by the Kremlin who should be protected or removed elsewhere."

Kennan's vision for political warfare was given top-secret approval and became NSC Directive 10/2.[16] This directive set up the Office of Special Projects (quickly renamed the Office of Policy Coordination). OPC activities were supposedly under the supervision of the CIA. In reality, from 1948 to 1952 the OPC was a law unto itself, engaging in a host of unconventional activities behind the Iron Curtain.[17]

U.S. Networking Efforts

American efforts to create anti-Communist networks were led by the OPC under Frank Wisner's leadership. In 1951, the network-building piece of the OPC was folded into the International Organization Division (IOD), an entire division of the CIA devoted to funding activities designed to influence European intelligentsia, students, and workers on both sides of the Iron Curtain.[18] Among the best known organizations supported by the IOD were the Congress of Cultural Freedom, RFE, RL, the Free Trade Union Committee (FTUC), and the National Stu-

---

[15] Policy Planning Staff, 1948.

[16] National Security Council, "National Security Council Directive on Office of Special Projects," NSC 10/2, June 18 1948, Record Group 273, Records of the National Security Council, NSC 10/2, National Archives and Records Administration.

[17] Evan Thomas, *The Very Best Men, Four Who Dared: The Early Years of the CIA*, New York: Simon & Schuster, 1995, pp. 29–30. In later years, Kennan became a major critic of U.S. foreign policy, arguing that his original conception of containment had been corrupted by a shift toward "militarization" of the conflict and the hardening of Europe into military alliances. However, at the time and in his private papers Kennan continued to support the political warfare activities he helped to launch, seeing them as a valuable tool in the United States' ideological conflict with the Soviet Union.

[18] Tom Braden, "I'm Glad the CIA Is 'Immoral,'" *Saturday Evening Post*, May 20, 1967.

dent Association (NSA), all of which were part of what Peter Coleman called the CIA's "liberal conspiracy."[19]

One important feature of this effort was the link between the public and private sectors. As historian Scott Lucas has noted, in these "state-private networks" often the impetus for the actions against Communism came from the private side of the equation.[20] Within the United States and Europe there already was an intellectual movement against Communism, particularly among the non-Communist left. However, money and organization were needed to turn individual efforts into a coherent campaign. The CIA did not create these networks out of thin air; they were born of wider cultural and political movements that the United States and other governments quietly fostered.

Liberation Committees

Most of the United States' networking activities in the late 1940s were focused on fostering democratic networks that could contest Communist domination of civil society in Western Europe. However, an important part of the general U.S. Cold War strategy was placing pressure on the Communist regimes in Eastern Europe and the Soviet Union through ideological warfare. The main organizations devoted to this cause were the NCFE, later called the Free Europe Committee (FEC), and the Amcomlib.

The establishment of the FEC was set in motion by OPC head Frank Wisner, who provided the initial funding for the project and assembled an amazing array of public figures to support the venture. It is important to note, however, that leading public figures of the time (such as John Foster Dulles and C.D. Jackson, then-General Dwight Eisenhower's chief advisor on psychological warfare during World War II) were already seeking ways to organize the Eastern European refugee community. The board of directors of FEC included future CIA Direc-

---

[19] Peter Coleman, *The Liberal Conspiracy: The Congress for Cultural Freedom and the Struggle for the Mind of Postwar Europe*, New York: Free Press, 1989.

[20] W. Scott Lucas, "Beyond Freedom, Beyond Control: Approaches to Cultural and the State-Private Network in the Cold War," *Intelligence and National Security*, Vol. 18, No. 2, Summer 2003, pp. 53–72.

tor Allen Dulles, publisher Henry Luce, General Lucius Clay, former ambassador to Japan Joseph Grew, and future-President Eisenhower.[21]

Initially, FEC activities were divided between three units. The first unit was exile relations. This unit helped organize exiles from Eastern Europe into an effective political force, which the FEC hoped would serve as a symbol of Eastern Europe's democratic future. As part of this process, the FEC found transitional jobs for exiled scholars in Western universities, launched a Free University in Strasbourg, France, to train the next generation of Eastern European leaders, and started a series of magazines analyzing developments in the Communist world.[22]

National committees were set up for each occupied country. These committees were made up of six or seven leading exile figures representing the political forces and interests of their respective countries before their occupation by the Soviet Union. The committees served as the liaison between the FEC and the émigré communities in the West, and their members became spokesmen and organizers of the exile community in the United States. This helped to maintain American and Western focus on the issue of Soviet occupation of Eastern Europe. Finally, the committees sponsored and helped to produce monthly magazines and journals in their native languages.[23]

The second set of FEC activities was organized by the division of American contacts. This unit was in charge of informing exiles about American culture and politics and promoting personal contacts between the exiles and the broader American public. This was part of a broad program to promote public support for American objectives at the beginning of the Cold War.[24]

---

[21] Arch Puddington, *Broadcasting Freedom: The Cold War Triumph of Radio Free Europe and Radio Liberty*, Lexington, Ky.: University Press of Kentucky, 2000, p. 12.

[22] Puddington, 2000, p. 12.

[23] The Baltic Committees are one example of these National Committees; see "Memorandum on Baltic Committees," November 29, 1955, Box 154, Baltic Committees, Radio Free Europe/Radio Liberty Corporate Archives, Hoover Institution Archives.

[24] "Excerpt from Minutes of Special Meeting of the Board of NCFE Directors," August 4, 1949, Box 286, Radio Free Europe Corporate Policy 1950–1956, Radio Free Europe/Radio Liberty Corporate Archives, Hoover Institution Archives.

An additional part of this effort was the Crusade for Freedom, which was officially launched by Dwight Eisenhower in a nationwide address on Labor Day in 1950.[25] The Crusade for Freedom was a fundraising activity to encourage the American public and corporations to contribute to the cause of freedom in the captive nations of Eastern Europe. In his speech, Eisenhower supplied the theme for the kickoff: "Fight the big lie with the big truth."[26] There was some hope that the Crusade for Freedom would provide the majority of funding for the FEC budget. Within a year or two, this proved to be impossible; the bulk of the FEC budget continued to come from the CIA. In later years, the Crusade for Freedom inspired a great deal of controversy as it was alleged that it was a cover for CIA funding of the FEC.[27]

The FEC's best-known and most important activity was RFE, which began broadcasting to the peoples of Eastern Europe over shortwave radio in 1950. RL, sponsored by Amcomlib, was similar to RFE but was broadcast in Russian (and other languages) and targeted the people of the Soviet Union. These stations provided an alternative news source for Communist bloc citizens. RFE and RL presented themselves to listeners as what a national radio station broadcasting from a free country would sound like. In addition to the news, they presented a full slate of broadcasts that included entertainment, cultural, and commentary programs. A mixed staff of Americans and émigrés housed in New York and Munich developed the content of the broadcasts.

While RFE and RL were largely funded by the CIA, they were very much independent entities that developed their own unique strategies for reaching their intended audiences. RL reached out to the Russian people by appealing to the democratic and humanitarian elements of their prerevolutionary tradition. It consistently emphasized the humanist aspects of Russian culture and history, such as the writing of Dostoyevsky and Tolstoy. In order to attract Soviet listeners, RL hired exiles who spoke Russian and other Soviet languages in a fluent and

---

[25] Martin J. Medhurst, "Eisenhower and the Crusade for Freedom: The Rhetorical Origins of a Cold War Campaign," *Presidential Studies Quarterly,* Vol. 27, Fall 1997, p. 649.

[26] Medhurst, 1997.

[27] Puddington, 2000, p. 22.

unaccented tone and used contemporary language in their broadcasts. It was hoped that RL would be viewed by Soviet citizens as a genuine expression of their aspiration for a democratic society.

By the 1960s, both RFE and RL had established themselves as trusted sources of information and commentary for the peoples of Eastern Europe and the Soviet Union. This trust became apparent when RFE and RL began receiving documents from internal dissenters inside the Communist bloc demanding civil liberties and religious freedom. RFE and RL broadcast readings of these texts, providing them with a wide circulation that they would never have received as strictly underground documents. RL was described as "a sounding board" on which Soviet citizens could express themselves and where they could exchange information.[28] By this time, RFE and RL, through their broadcasts, had become major players in the political, cultural, and philosophical debates going on inside the Communist bloc.

FEC and Amcomlib also sponsored book-mailing programs that distributed publications to Eastern Europe and the Soviet Union. George Minden, head of the Free Europe Press, established a book-mailing program for Eastern Europe that distributed materials that provided a "spiritual understanding of Western values."[29] Minden tried to avoid politics in his book selections, focusing instead on sending materials on "psychology, literature, the theatre, and visuals arts" to Eastern European intellectuals and thinkers.[30] Free Europe Press was able to secure the foreign language rights to many classic works from Western publishers for a very small fee. This book-mailing program concentrated on books that were either banned or not available in the Communist bloc, which more often than not got past Communist censors when they came from legitimate Western institutions or publishers. It distributed books such as James Joyce's *Portrait of the Artist as a Young Man*, Vladimir Nabokov's *Prin*, George Orwell's *Animal*

---

[28] Gene Sosin, *Sparks of Liberty: An Insider's Memoir of Radio Liberty*, University Park, Pa.: Pennsylvania State University Press, 1999, p. 152 .

[29] John P.C. Matthews, "The West's Secret Marshall Plan for the Mind," *International Journal of Intelligence and Counter Intelligence*," Vol. 16, No. 3, July–September 2003.

[30] Matthews, 2003.

Farm, and later Robert Conquest's famous book on Stalin's purges, *The Great Terror*.[31] By the end of the Cold War it was estimated that over ten million Western books and magazines had infiltrated the Communist half of Europe through the book-mailing programs.[32]

Congress of Cultural Freedom

One of the most important anti-Communist organizations of the Cold War was the Congress of Cultural Freedom, founded in 1950. The original idea for the congress came from a group of European and American intellectuals, including Melvin Lasky and Ruth Fisher, in the summer of 1949. They wanted to hold an international conference in Berlin to unify opposition to Stalinism in Western and Eastern Europe. They envisioned the conference as a response to a series of Soviet-sponsored conferences calling for world peace and denouncing the policies of the Truman administration, one of which was held in New York and attended by 800 prominent literary and artistic figures including Arthur Miller, Aaron Copland, Charlie Chaplin, and Albert Einstein.[33]

Plans for what would ultimately become the Congress of Cultural Freedom remained in bureaucratic limbo for some time. American authorities in Germany likely knew about the plans but were concerned that a conference sponsored by the U.S. government would have little credibility with European intellectuals. Into this breach stepped two pivotal figures: Michael Josselson and Melvin Lasky.

Michael Josselson, who was born in Estonia but became an American citizen, was a cultural affairs officer with the American Military Government of Germany. He liked the idea of a conference and had grand plans for it. Josselson wanted to hold a cultural and intellectual conference that would seize the initiative from the Communists by reaffirming "the fundamental ideals governing cultural and politi-

---

[31] Matthews, 2003.

[32] Matthews, 2003.

[33] Coleman, 1989, p. 5.

cal action in the Western world and the repudiation of all totalitarian challenges."[34]

Josselson proposed to the OPC that a committee of American and European intellectuals organize the conference and invite the participants. The participants would be selected on the basis of three criteria: their political outlook, their international reputation, and their popularity in Germany. The purpose of Congress would be to found a permanent committee, which, with a bit of funding, would maintain a degree of intellectual and rhetorical coordination. The OPC liked Josselson's plan and approved a budget of $50,000 for it.

Melvin Lasky was also instrumental in getting the conference off the ground. Lasky was the American journalist who had founded *Der Monat,* a German journal sponsored by the American occupation authorities. During this period the United States and its allies were actively engaged in trying to reconstruct German institutions and culture and controlled licensing for German publications. *Der Monat* was an enormous success and made Lasky a major intellectual and cultural figure in Europe.[35]

After hearing of Josselson's interest in the conference plan, Lasky leaped into action. This was of some concern to the OPC, which worried that Lasky, an employee of the American occupation government, would be pointed to as proof that the U.S. government was behind the event.[36] Lasky would not be deterred, however, and in a whirlwind of activity he managed to enlist the mayor of West Berlin and a host of prominent intellectuals for the conference.

The Congress of Cultural Freedom opened in Berlin on June 26, 1950, the day after North Korean forces launched their invasion of South Korea. The congress was marked by differing views on how to oppose Communism. One group favored a militant frontal assault,

---

[34] Michael Warner, "Origins of the Congress of Cultural Freedom 1949–1950," *Studies in Intelligence,* Vol. 38, No. 5, 1995.

[35] Giles Scott-Smith, "A Radical Democratic Political Offensive: Melvin J. Lasky, *Der Monat,* and the Congress of Cultural Freedom," *Journal of Contemporary History,* Vol. 35, No. 2, 2000, pp. 263–280.

[36] Warner, 1995; Scott-Smith, 2000.

while others wanted a more subtle, less confrontational approach that focused on social and political reforms in order to undermine Communism's moral appeal. Despite these differences, the congress agreed to a manifesto rejecting neutralism, calling for peace through the establishment of democratic institutions, and expressing solidarity with the victims of totalitarian states.[37] The congress also agreed to set up a permanent organization to advocate the principles agreed upon in Berlin.

The Berlin conference set out the underlying purpose of the Congress of Cultural Freedom that would sustain it over seventeen years. The congress aimed to form a trans-Atlantic, anti-totalitarian consensus based upon the universal values of free thought and enquiry. National committees were formed throughout Europe (and later in Asia and Latin America). Each committee was composed of independent intellectuals who sponsored activities that they believed were appropriate to advance the general principles of the congress. One of the main activities of the national committees was the publication of magazines and journals.

The best-known publication sponsored by the congress was *Encounter*, co-edited by Irving Kristol and Stephen Spender and published in London. *Encounter* was sponsored by the congress but was not published directly by it; it was also independent of the British Society of Cultural Freedom. An intellectual review that covered international cultural and political trends from a British perspective, *Encounter* solicited content from a mix of British, American, and European writers.

The congress produced over a dozen intellectual reviews around the world in English, French, Spanish, and German. Each of these magazines had a similar liberal, anti-Communist viewpoint and covered cultural as well as political issues. In the 1950s and early 1960s several of these magazines became the most discussed and talked about journals in their respective countries.

The Congress of Cultural Freedom also held international conferences on major political and social issues. Their goal was to create an international forum for debate, not merely another instrument in the ideological struggle against the Soviet Union. The congress sought

---

[37] Coleman, 1989, p. 31.

to provide constructive viewpoints on social, political, and economic behavior that were not merely reflexively anti-Communist.[38] These conferences became the focus of trans-Atlantic intellectual debate on modernization, democracy, and technological development. For example, a 1955 conference provided a forum for a debate between the economists J. K. Galbraith and Friedrich von Hayek about the proper role of government in the economy and whether state control over the economy had any relationship to political freedom.

The congress was also politically active, organizing protests against the oppression of intellectuals in both left-wing and right-wing dictatorships. After the Soviets suppressed the Hungarian revolution in 1956, the congress mobilized worldwide support for Hungarian writers, artists, and scientists. The congress provided assistance to the Hungarian refugees that fled the country, particularly the intellectuals among them. It also protested the Franco regime's suspension of professors in Spain in 1965 and the arrest by Portuguese authorities in Mozambique of an anti-colonial editor in 1965.[39]

The CIA assisted the Congress of Cultural Freedom in two ways. The first was to supply funding. After the Berlin conference, the congress wanted to continue its activities but had no reliable source of funds. The congress was unlikely to receive money from the Department of State or the U.S. Congress. This was the period of the McCarthy hearings; in such an environment it was difficult for a left-of-center group to obtain overt funding from the U.S. government. The CIA, on the other hand, was both willing and able to fund liberal anti-Communist organizations. CIA funding was kept secret in order for the congress to maintain credibility with its membership; many of these European intellectuals were unlikely to cooperate with a group directly receiving funding from the U.S. government.

The second role the CIA played in the success of the congress was ensuring that it had competent and loyal leadership. In Novem-

---

[38] Giles Scott-Smith, "The Congress for Cultural Freedom, the End of Ideology and the 1955 Milan Conference: Defining the Parameters of Discourse," *Journal of Contemporary History*, Vol. 37, No. 3, 2002, pp. 437–455.

[39] Coleman, 1989, p. 244.

ber 1950, the OPC choose Michael Josselson for the position of the congress's administrative secretary, a role he would fulfill for the next sixteen years.[40] Josselson resigned his job with the American occupation government in Germany in order to take the new position. Josselson thus held two positions within the congress: he was both an organizer of a worldwide community of intellectuals and a link to the organization's funding source, the CIA.

Labor Unions

In the late 1940s, Communist forces held a dominant position in the labor movement throughout Europe and Asia. Even in North America, the Congress of Industrial Organizations (CIO), one of the leading U.S. labor organizations, included prominent Communists among its first generation of leaders. Their dominance was centered on the Communist-controlled World Federation of Trade Unions (WFTU), established in 1945. In contraposition to the Communist trade union movement was the American Federation of Labor (AFL), under the leadership of George Meany. The AFL established the FTUC to assist free trade unions abroad, particularly in Europe. The FTUC was headed by Jay Lovestone, an ex-Communist who had turned against the party after being expelled for demanding some degree of independence for American Communist trade union groups in the late 1920s. Lovestone and Meany shared a vision of a global trade-union movement that was free of Communist control and that respected the rules of a free-market economy.[41]

In 1945, Lovestone sent Irving Brown to Paris to establish a European FTUC office in order to build up non-Communist unions in France and Italy. The FTUC conducted a range of operations, including financially supporting anti-Communist labor publications; materially supporting non-Communist trade unions; systematically attempting to woo dissident Communist Party members in France and Italy; providing organizational assistance and courier services for the Con-

---

[40] Warner, 1995.

[41] Anthony Carew, *Labour Under the Marshall Plan: The Politics of Productivity and the Marketing of Management Science*, Detroit, Mich.: Wayne State University Press, 1987.

gress for Cultural Freedom; and establishing a network of undercover agents in Eastern Europe. Beyond Europe, the FTUC mounted anti-Communist programs targeted on the labor movements in India, Indonesia, and Taiwan.[42]

FTUC activities were funded by the AFL, American corporations, and the Department of State. The approval of the Marshall Plan in 1948 put the FTUC on firmer financial footing; the plan stipulated that five percent of funds should be used for administrative purposes and rebuilding Western European unions.[43] The OPC/CIA did not become involved with the FTUC until 1949, when agreement was reached between the OPC and the FTUC that the CIA would fund specific FTUC projects. As money for the Marshall Plan decreased, the FTUC became increasingly dependent upon the CIA for financing.[44]

In 1949, under prodding from the U.S. government, the CIO purged its Communist leadership and withdrew from the WFTU. This provided the spark for the AFL and the CIO to jointly participate in the creation of the International Confederation of Free Trade Unions (ICFTU), a global anti-Communist organization with member unions in 53 countries.[45] The WFTU was now left with membership drawn only from Communist-controlled labor groups, greatly diminishing the influence of the organization.

The relationship between the U.S. government and the FTUC was not smooth; there were strong and consistent disagreements, particularly between the FTUC and the CIA. These conflicts centered around two fundamental disagreements. The first arose over basic Cold War strategy and the role the labor movement should play therein. The Department of State and the CIO believed that economic and social hardships opened the door to Communism, and felt that resisting Communism required polices that addressed broad social and

---

[42] Anthony Carew, "The American Labor Movement in Fizzland: The Free Trade Union Committee and the CIA," *Labour History*, Vol. 39, No. 4, February 1998.

[43] Scott Lucas, *Freedom's War: The American Crusade Against the Soviet Union*, New York: New York University Press, 1999, p. 46.

[44] Carew, 1998.

[45] The AFL and CIO formally merged into the AFL-CIO in 1955.

economic issues.[46] The FTUC rejected this viewpoint, believing that workers were more interested in freedom than bread and butter issues; in their view Communism had an appeal that reached beyond purely economic issues. Combating Communism, according to the FTUC, required directly challenging it in all avenues of society. For the labor movement this meant engaging in a variety of actions that directly undermined Communist unions and promoted alternative, non-Communist ones.[47] Along with the increasing role the CIO played in the international labor movement, these conflicting strategic viewpoints created friction between the FTUC and the CIA throughout the early Cold War period.

The other area of disagreement between the CIA and the FTUC concerned the question of who should be in charge of funds distribution. Lovestone, Brown, and others openly questioned CIA labor policy in Europe. Lovestone regarded the CIA's Ivy League–educated officers as amateurs when it came to fighting Communism in the labor movement, dismissing them as "Fizz Kids."[48] He wanted the CIA to provide the FTUC with bloc grants and to allow the FTUC to conduct operations as it saw fit. The CIA, on the other hand, saw the FTUC as too assertive and out of control. Despite their tempestuous relationship, the CIA continued to support the FTUC until 1957, when the U.S. Agency for International Development (USAID) began funding labor activities overseas.

Student Organizations

Perhaps the most controversial of the U.S. government's network-building activities was its role in funding the NSA, whose covert activities were revealed by the magazine *Ramparts* in 1967.[49] These revelations

---

[46] Anthony Carew, "The Politics of Productivity and the Politics of Anti-Communism: American and European Labour in the Cold War," *Intelligence and National Security,* Vol. 18, No. 2, Summer 2003, pp. 73–91.

[47] Carew, 2003.

[48] Carew, 1998.

[49] Michael Warner, "Sophisticated Spies: CIA's Links to Liberal Anti-Communists 1949–1967," *International Journal of Intelligence and Counter Intelligence*, Vol. 9, No. 4, Winter 1996/1997, p. 425.

led to more investigations, which in turn uncovered dozens of other similar covert operations run by the CIA's IOD. Among the relationships exposed was the CIA's support of the Congress of Cultural Freedom and its ties to union groups. This publicity effectively ended the CIA's covert attempts to challenge Soviet front organizations in sectors such as youth, labor, intellectuals, artists, journalists, and academics.

The CIA had become involved in youth organizations for many of the same reasons it became involved in other areas of civil society. In the late 1940s, the Soviet Union had a monopoly on international organizations devoted to students and youth. The World Federation of Democratic Youth (WFDY) and the International Union of Students (IUS), the only two international youth and student organizations recognized by the United Nations, were effectively Soviet front organizations. The WFDY and the IUS toed the Stalinist line, attacking the Marshall Plan, backing North Korea's invasion of South Korea, and supporting Stalin's peace offensive.[50]

The WFDY sponsored youth and student festivals that brought hundreds of thousands of students from Africa, Asia, and Europe to what were billed as cultural and social events. However, these festivals were highly political, presenting the Communist version of current events and displaying life in Communist countries in the best light possible. Vast sums of money were spent hosting the festivals. For example, in 1951 the East German government spent $48 million staging the Third World Youth and Student Festival in Berlin.[51]

Western efforts to counter Communist youth and student groups were limited prior to 1950. In 1947, the NSA was formed in Madison, Wisconsin. Initially a member of Communist-controlled IUS, the NSA broke with that organization in 1948 over its failure to condemn the Communist coup in Czechoslovakia. The NSA's attempts to found a rival international student organization foundered due to lack of organizational skills and money. With some limited financial help from the Department of State and the CIA, British, Swedish, and American

---

[50] Joel Kotek, "Youth Organizations as a Battlefield in the Cold War," *Intelligence and National Security*, Vol. 18, No. 2, Summer 2003, pp. 168–191.

[51] Kotek, 2003.

student groups managed to hold a meeting of student organizations dissatisfied with the IUS in Stockholm, Sweden, in 1950.[52]

After the Stockholm conference, the CIA became more involved in NSA efforts, providing the organization with funding that allowed it to reach out to student groups in Latin America, Asia, and the Middle East. This led to the creation of the International Student Conference (ISC) in 1952. However, the CIA did not finance NSA directly, instead funneling money to the group through private organizations such as the Rockefeller and Ford Foundations.[53] ISC offices were set up in several countries to support the movement of funds. By the mid-1950s, the ISC had become a leading provider of international youth programs involving technical assistance, education, and student exchanges and scholarships that allowed third-world students to study in the West.[54]

Role of U.S. Government Foundation-Like

In almost all of these endeavors the U.S. government acted like a foundation. It evaluated projects to determine whether they promoted U.S. objectives, provided funding for them, and then adopted a hands-off approach, allowing the organizations it supported to fulfill their objectives without interference. Like any foundation, the U.S. government set out guidelines for how its money was to be spent. However, U.S. officials generally realized that the greater the distance between their government and the sponsored organization, the more likely the organization's activities would succeed.

The U.S. government supported network-building activities during the Cold War in four vital ways. The first was helping to organize democratic network-building groups. As documented in the examples above, the level of planning and organization provided by U.S.-government agencies varied greatly depending upon the group

---

[52] Karen Paget, "From Stockholm to Leiden: The CIA's Role in the Formation of the International Student Conference," *Intelligence and National Security*, Vol. 18, No. 2, Summer 2003, pp. 134–167.

[53] Kotek, 2003.

[54] Sol Stern, "A Short Account of International Student Politics, and the Cold War with Particular Reference to the NSA, CIA, etc.," *Ramparts*, Vol. 5, No. 9, March 1967, pp. 29–38.

they were supporting. In some cases, such as U.S. support for union activities in Europe, the government played a very minor role in the actual organization of the groups. This was because private groups, in this case the AFL, had already established an effective network on their own. In other cases, such as that of the Congress of Cultural Freedom, U.S. government officials played a much larger role. The Congress of Cultural Freedom only came into being because U.S. officials turned a set of ideas, put forward by scattered individuals, into a concrete plan for action.

The second area of U.S.-government support was financial. Funding was generally provided through foundations, which maintained a degree of distance between the government and the organizations it was supporting. Although only a small number of individuals within each organization knew about the U.S. government's role as a source of funds, it was not a secret. Since the opening of Communist archives, it has been well documented that Soviet-bloc regimes were aware that the CIA was involved in funding these organizations. While some organizations were able to raise private funding for their efforts, these funds were never sufficient to support the full range of the groups' activities. U.S. government support was instrumental in allowing these organizations to compete on a level playing field with Communist-front organizations, which of course were well funded by Communist regimes.

A third area of U.S. network-building support was general policy guidance. For example, former RL staff members described the organization's policy development process as a joint effort between RL, the CIA, and the Department of State. RL staff would write the general policy guidelines, and then they would be sent to the CIA and the Department of State for coordination.[55] During the 1950s, an interagency group called the Committee on Radio Broadcasting provided the framework for this coordination process. In a 1958 memorandum, the committee laid out the practices and policies RL was to follow. The memo covers a range of subjects, including the objectives of U.S.

---

[55] Author's interviews with former staff members Gene Sosin (interviewed at home in Westchester, New York, April 2005), Jim Critchlow (interviewed by telephone, July 2005), and Ross Johnson (interviewed at RFE/RL Corporate Headquarters, June 2005).

information programs, the organization of the stations, and general approaches and techniques to use.[56] In other cases, such as with the Congress of Cultural Freedom, the U.S. government played a very limited role in providing policy guidance.

The final role of the U.S. government in building networks was to provide organizations with limited direct assistance. In some cases, this meant having CIA staff serve as personal assistants to the heads of the organizations, which kept the government fully informed about organizations' ongoing activities and effectiveness. Another avenue of direct U.S. government assistance involved directly influencing critical staff appointments. The U.S. government vetted and approved the heads of all of the major organizations, ensuring that in most cases the leaders of these organizations were well-respected private individuals with a previous history of public service.

While the direct role of the U.S. government in building an anti-Communist network was substantial, it is perhaps more important to highlight the things left to the leadership of the individual organizations. Because these leaders were trusted individuals, they were given the flexibility to develop strategies and tactics best suited to their missions. This encouraged the development of a great variety of strategies, which often were needed for the very different network-building tasks at hand. With the exception of the highest level of leadership, each organization hired its own employees and decided who would and would not participate in the activities they sponsored. This political flexibility allowed the organizations to work with individuals and groups that normally would not have been associated with activities supported by the U.S. government. Finally, the organizations ran their own day-to-day affairs. According to declassified documents, the CIA believed that network-building organizations were most effective when they were given the widest autonomy possible.[57]

---

[56] "Gray Broadcasting Policy Toward the Soviet Union," May 1, 1958. Appendices to Memorandum for the President from the Director of Central Intelligence, declassified for Conference on Cold War Broadcasting Impact, Stanford, Calif., October 13–15, 2004, Document Reader.

[57] Cord Meyer, who headed the CIA's IOD from 1954 to the early 1970s, wrote about the hands-off relationship between the CIA and the organizations it funded in his book *Facing*

British Network-Building Activities

The United States was not the only nation engaged in network-building activities at the beginning of the Cold War. In early 1948, the British government set up the Information Research Department (IRD), a secret part of the Foreign Office, to oversee British Cold War propaganda efforts. The IRD was guided by the principle that people in free countries would reject Soviet Communism if they understood the real conditions in Communist-controlled countries and the aims and methods of Soviet propaganda. To do this the IRD embarked on "worldwide operation of factual indoctrination" to counter Soviet propaganda.[58]

The IRD surveyed the structures of various communities both inside and outside Britain in order to identify opinion leaders willing to cooperate with the British government in combating Communism. The IRD was particularly interested in religious figures, union leaders, intellectuals, and journalists. Individuals from these groups were confidentially supplied with background materials about Communism and life in the Soviet Union from open sources and from British intelligence, enabling them to speak knowledgeably on the subject. These nonofficial figures could promote the anti-Communist message without appearing to be sponsored or endorsed by the British government.

The IRD also purchased the foreign publications rights of books and articles it thought would be particularly useful in undermining Communism. George Orwell was an early recruit of the IRD and allowed the organization to translate his novels *Animal Farm* and *1984* into eighteen different languages, including Finnish, Latvian, and Ukrainian. The IRD also established a network of journalists, both foreign and domestic, willing to use IRD materials in their stories. For example, in 1949 the IRD undertook a complex, three-pronged

---

Reality: From World Federation to the CIA. No documents or interviews contradicting his characterization of these relationships have emerged since Meyer published his book in 1980. Cord Meyer, *Facing Reality: From World Federalism to the CIA,* New York: Harper & Row, 1980.

[58] Ralph Murray, "Progress Report on the Work of the IRD," memorandum to Christopher Warner, March 21, 1950. Foreign Office 1110/359/PR110/5, Public Record Office, United Kingdom.

press operation to expose the Soviet slave labor camps. First, a government minister disclosed on the floor of the House of Commons the discovery of a Codex book outlining the operation of Soviet slave labor camps. The IRD alerted the BBC Overseas Service to the existence of the document prior to the minister's statement and the subsequent release of the document. In addition, friendly members of the British and foreign press were notified about the statement in advance in order to allow them to prepare stories for publication. Coverage of the story was extensive, and the information about Soviet labor practices was published in over fifty countries and broadcast by the BBC Overseas Service in numerous languages.

Lessons from the Cold War Experience

As discussed in the introduction, the United States faces a number of challenges in constructing democratic networks in the Muslim world. Many of these challenges mirror those faced by policymakers at the beginning of the Cold War. In this section, we briefly analyze how Cold War–era policymakers dealt with some of them.

Should the U.S. Network-Building Efforts Be Offensive or Defensive? In the late 1940s and early 1950s, U.S. and British policymakers debated whether they should pursue an offensive or defensive strategy when confronting the Soviet Union. The defensive strategy was focused on "containing" the Soviet threat by bolstering democratic forces in Western Europe (and later in Latin America, Asia, and the Middle East) to ensure they could resist pressure from Communist forces. Others advocated an offensive strategy known as both "liberation" and "rollback." Liberation policy was focused on destroying Communist rule in Eastern Europe and ultimately within the Soviet Union itself. Network-building efforts under this strategy focused on aiding, both overtly and covertly, groups inside Eastern Europe and the Soviet Union that were actively engaged in attempts to overthrow Communist governments.

For the most part, the defensive strategy of containment prevailed in both the United States and Britain for several reasons. First, after the failure of efforts to support resistance groups within the Soviet bloc, policymakers concluded that their capability to influence the internal dynamics of Communist societies was extremely limited. Only the governments and people of Communist countries, not an outside power, could overturn the Communists' control of Eastern Europe and the Soviet Union. Second, any active association between the West and groups inside the Communist bloc would result in the violent repression of those groups. Third, bolstering democratic networks in Western Europe both stabilized the society there and established channels to reverse the flow of ideas—instead of Communist ideas flowing into Western Europe via the Soviet Union and its front organizations, democratic ideas could infiltrate behind the Iron Curtain via the newly established networks.

How to Maintain the Credibility of Groups Receiving Outside Support? The concern that U.S. backing would discredit democratic organizations was substantial during the Cold War, as it is today. Policymakers in the late 1940s and early 1950s attempted to avoid this pitfall by keeping their support covert. The United States funded the organizations through foundations, both real and fictional. Initially, only a limited number of individuals knew about the covert backing of the new democratic organizations, and thus they avoided the negative repercussions of U.S. support for a time. But, as is almost always the case, the covert U.S. support was ultimately revealed. Once this occurred, the credibility of these organizations was compromised, and many never recovered.

The credibility of the organizations was better maintained by providing a degree of real distance between the groups and the U.S. government, for example by supporting the efforts of private and nongovernmental organizations with established relationships in the countries in which they operated. Another way of quietly influencing organizations while maintaining their credibility was through the appointment of reputable public figures as movement leaders. The reputations of these leaders lent the groups a degree of credibility that helped to mitigate any concerns about potential ties to the U.S. government.

Finally, it is important to note that many individuals and organizations were happy to accept U.S. government funding. They fully understood the political and personal danger that came from accepting outside support. However, they believed in their cause and wanted to exploit every available advantage.

How Broad a Coalition? At the beginning of the Cold War, the United States faced a dilemma in scoping its anti-Communist coalition. On one hand, the U.S. government sought to form a broad coalition across the political spectrum in order to demonstrate the limited appeal of Communism. On the other hand, it also wanted to restrict its support to groups that adhered to a set of basic principles, which could be summarized as the acceptance of liberal democratic values, including fundamental individual and political rights.

The organizers of the West's network-building effort came to the conclusion that as long as groups and individuals accepted these principles they were welcomed into the fight against Communism, no matter where they lay on the political spectrum. Organizations supported financially by the U.S. government were allowed (and even encouraged) to disagree with U.S. policies. Many in the U.S. government believed that the credibility and independence of these organizations, particularly those individuals and groups on the left of the political spectrum, were enhanced by their expression of genuine disagreement with U.S. policies. The Congress of Cultural Freedom, RFE, and RL all believed that the most effective criticism of the Soviet regime came not from the right, which was to be expected, but from the non-Communist left, including individuals who had only recently abandoned the Communist party. The head of RL imparted this wisdom to his employees, saying, "a left hook to the Kremlin is the best blow."[59]

Should the United States Become Involved in Internal Ideological Issues? Communists often had extended debates about the true meaning of Marxism as it relates to economic, political, and social policy. These debates often highlighted the conflict between reformers, who wanted to make alterations to the Stalinist economic and social model, and hardliners, who opposed reform. From the Western perspective, the reformers were clearly preferable to the hardliners. However, it was unclear how much encouragement the West should provide

---

[59] Lowell Schwartz interview with Gene Sosin, April 2005.

to the reformers, who, in spite of their reform efforts, at the end of the day wanted to preserve the Communist system.

While no clear consensus on this question emerged, a few rules were generally applied. Reforms that improved the lives of the population were always applauded. However, this applause was always followed by a statement indicating that these reforms had not gone far enough in correcting the problem, which stemmed from the very nature of Communism. In general, Western groups tried not to engage in the interpretation of Marxist ideology; engaging in internal Marxist philosophical debates only took time and attention away from the important task of highlighting the fundamental differences between totalitarian and free societies.

Religion, however, was very much part of the Western discourse. Extensive efforts were made to explain the role of religion in a free society and that people in the West were free to worship in any way they chose, which included the freedom not to worship at all. The importance of religion in responding to ethical and moral questions was also addressed; RFE and RL each broadcast religion programs on Sunday discussing questions people confronted in their daily lives.

Why Was the Effort Successful?

U.S. and Western network-building activities are now regarded as one of the key reasons for the West's victory in the Cold War. The success of these efforts can broadly be attributed to several factors. First, the development of democratic networks was closely tied to a grand strategy that incorporated all aspects of national power short of war, including political, economic, informational, and diplomatic components. Second, U.S. networking efforts tapped into movements and organizations that already existed in Western Europe. Government assistance was a vital complement in nurturing this movement; however, care had to be taken not to overshadow it or crush it with attention.

Moreover, there was a broad political consensus inside the United States and in some allied countries, notably Great Britain, on the need to fight Communism in its political and ideological, as well as military, manifestations. This consensus lasted for almost twenty years, allowing both overt and covert support for networking efforts to continue without domestic political interference. This was despite the fact that many journalists, lawmakers, and intellectuals were well aware of covert funding for some of these programs.

Finally, the U.S. government managed to strike a balance that allowed the groups it supported a high level of independence while ensuring that their activities converged with long-term U.S. strategic goals. The creative, credible, and flexible efforts of these organizations would never have been possible under constant U.S.-government supervision.

CHAPTER THREE

Parallels Between the Cold War and the Challenges in the Muslim World Today

Three broad parallels stand out between the Cold War environment and the challenges that the United States and the West face in the Muslim world today. First, as in the late 1940s, the United States is currently confronted with a new and confusing geopolitical environment with new security threats. During the 1940s, the threat came from the Soviet Union and was compounded by the devastating potential of attacks with nuclear weapons. A rival superpower, the Soviet Union supported and was supported by client states and an international movement driven by an inimical ideology, a movement that assisted the Soviet Union in attacking Western democracy through overt and covert means. Today, the United States and its allies face the threat of an ideologically driven global jihadist movement striking with acts of mass-casualty terrorism and seeking to overturn the international order.

Another parallel lies in the creation of large new government bureaucracies to combat these threats. The NSC, the Department of Defense, and the CIA were all established in 1947 as the United States prepared for its new role as the leader of the Western camp. In 2002, the Department of Homeland Security was created to combat the threat to the United States posed by international terrorists, and new programs such as the Middle East Partnership Initiative (MEPI) were launched to shape the environment in the Middle East. There was also a recognition of the need to reorient the U.S. intelligence establishment to more effectively confront these new threats; in 2004, Congress approved the largest reorganization of the national intelligence community since the inception of the CIA.

Finally, and most importantly for this project, during the early Cold War years there was a recognition that the United States and its allies were engaged in an ideological conflict between liberal democracy and Communism. Policymakers understood this ideological conflict would be contested across diplomatic, economic, military, and psychological dimensions. It was a battle for the hearts and minds of a variety of audiences; among the most important were the general public both behind the Iron Curtain and in Western Europe. Today, as recognized by the Defense Department in its *Quadrennial Defense Review Report*, the United States is involved in a war that is "both a battle of arms and a battle of ideas," a war in which ultimate victory will be achieved only "when extremist ideologies are discredited in the eyes of their host populations and tacit supporters."[1]

Of course, as with all historical analogies, it is important to note key differences as well as the similarities between the past and the present. As a nation-state, the Soviet Union had state interests to protect, defined geographical borders, and a clear government structure. This meant the Soviet Union could be deterred from certain actions, such as attacking the United States or its allies, through the threat of military retaliation against its military, leadership, and population. It was also possible to negotiate with the Soviets, and, at least in later years, the Soviet Union behaved much like any other nation-state, seeking to maximize its power and prestige in the international system.

In the Global War on Terrorism, the United States is confronting a very different type of enemy: shadowy non-state actors that are not subject to traditional means of deterrence. As they control no territory (although some have been able to establish sanctuaries outside of state control), it is unclear what targets, if any, the United States could hold at risk to deter attack. Our current adversaries' strategic objectives are often unclear, and they reject the norms of the international system.

---

[1]   U.S. Department of Defense, *Quadrennial Defense Review Report*, February 6, 2006, pp. 21–22.

Table 3.1 summarizes the key differences between the Cold War environment and the environment in the Muslim world today.

The first difference highlighted in Table 3.1 relates to the role of civil society. Historically, civil-society institutions have been very strong in Western Europe; during the Cold War the United States had a foundation upon which to build democratic networks. In the Muslim world—particularly in the Middle East—the institutions of civil society are in the process of developing, making the task of building democratic networks more difficult.

Intellectual and historical ties were, of course, stronger between Europe and the United States. American political culture has its roots in Europe, in British constitutional and legal development, and in the ideas of the Enlightenment. These shared experiences and values made it easier for the United States to engage in a war of ideas. While Western liberal ideas have taken root in some countries and among some sectors in the Muslim world—perhaps more than is generally appreciated—the cultural and historical divide between the United States and

Table 3.1
Networking Challenges: The Cold War and the Middle East Today

	Cold War	Middle East (Today)
Role of civil society	Historically strong	Historically not strong but developing
Hostility between United States and targeted society/ government	Open hostility between Soviet Union and United States Western societies favorable United States seen as liberator in Western Europe	U.S. democracy promotion and moderate network building is seen by authoritarian U.S. Middle East security partners as destabilizing United States not seen as liberator
Intellectual and historical ties	Strong	Weak
Adversary's ideology	Secular	Religion based
Nature of opposing networks	Centrally controlled	Loose or no central control
Policy challenges	Less complex	More complex

its potential moderate Muslim partners is greater than that between the United States and Europe during the Cold War.

Today's information environment is also very different. During the Cold War, the media was made up of a limited number of newspapers, magazines, and radio and television stations. Today, the media environment in the Middle East is far more complex, with traditional state-run media outlets being challenged by the Internet and hundreds of satellite television stations. Unlike during the Cold War, when the central challenge, particularly in Eastern Europe, was communicating truthful information that was being suppressed by totalitarian governments, the challenge today is countering the messages of a proliferation of media that promote and validate sectarian and extremist worldviews.

Nevertheless, as one of our reviewers points out, these differences and difficulties do not preclude useful work in this area. The Muslim world is in very great need of the habits of self-examination, self-reflection, and self-criticism, all of which require reliable access to and appreciation of factual information. To influence the intellectual environment in the Muslim World this goal is certainly a complicated matter and would require a sophisticated approach, but it is not unlike the effort the United States made during the Cold War—the steady supply of factual information was an important factor in shaping opinion. Similarly, by supplying a platform for debate, the United States was able to show that certain views were "debatable." The problem is not that these things cannot be done again, but that they have not even been tried.[2]

The operating environment today is dangerous in a very different way than it was during the Cold War. Members of democratic networks, particularly defectors from the Communist bloc, were often targeted by Communist intelligence agencies. However, the Soviets were somewhat inhibited from targeting individuals working directly with the United States and U.S. personnel because of the possibility of retaliation against their own operatives. Today, terrorists operate out-

---

[2]   Hilled Fradkin, review of report, October 2006.

side of any norms or limits and have shown a strong willingness to target any individual or institution that they regard as an enemy.

Another key difference is the complexity of political choices faced by the United States today. During the Cold War, the political choices for the United States were clear-cut—the United States defended its friends and opposed the Soviet Union and its allies. In the Muslim world today the choices are much more complex; to a large extent criticism of the United States is focused on U.S. ties to authoritarian regimes. The dilemma for U.S. policy is that the promotion of democracy may undermine governments that are part of the current security structure that the United States supports in the region.

CHAPTER FOUR

U.S. Government Efforts to Stem the Radical Tide

The terrorist attacks of September 11, 2001, served as a catalyst for a reassessment and readjustment of U.S. national-security programs. Initially, a great deal of resources and attention were devoted to the physical security of American citizens and territory. Consequent government spending increases and organizational restructuring were designed to bolster the capacity and effectiveness of U.S. military, intelligence, and law enforcement activities. This eventually resulted in the establishment of the Department of Homeland Security and fundamental changes to the intelligence community.

At the same time, with the recognition that combating terrorism was not only a matter of bringing terrorists to justice and diminishing their capacity to operate, there was an effort to understand and address the deeper sources of terrorism. The National Security Strategy document of September 2002 elucidated a refined conception of security that emphasized the consequences of internal conditions of other states: "America will encourage the advancement of democracy and economic openness . . . because these are the best foundations for domestic stability and international order." This theme was to be reinforced over the course of the next several years, from the 9/11 Commission Report to, perhaps most dramatically, President Bush's second inaugural address.[1]

---

[1] This trend was evident most recently in the updated National Security Strategy document, issued in March 2006, which put the promotion of democracy and freedom as the "first pillar:" "The first pillar is promoting freedom, justice, and human dignity—working to end tyranny, to promote effective democracies, and to extend prosperity through free and

The elevation of the President's "Freedom Agenda" in rhetoric has raised expectations that the past U.S. national-security policy of promoting stability had changed sufficiently to pose challenges to autocratic and repressive regimes. In practice, however, the promotion of freedom and democracy represent, at best, incremental steps that rarely have involved explicit challenges to illiberal regimes. While there are promising indications of reform reflected in greater freedom of expression and the growth of pro-democracy nongovernmental organizations (NGOs) in the Muslim world, key allies in the "war on terror" such as Egypt and Pakistan have shown very little tangible progress toward liberal democratic outcomes.[2]

From its prominence in a series of high-profile documents and speeches, the Freedom Agenda can be considered to be a U.S. "grand strategy." However, there has yet to emerge a definitive annunciation of related foreign-policy goals, consistent identification of allies in the "war of ideas," and tactics for enlisting them in a comprehensive campaign.[3] Consequently, the relationship between the building of moderate Muslim networks and the security components of the "war on terrorism" remains unclear. Moreover, the short-term security goal of degrading terrorist capacity and the long-term goal of promoting democracy can appear to conflict, especially with relation to U.S. cooperation with friendly, but authoritarian, states on security issues.

---

fair trade and wise development policies." The White House, "Fact Sheet: The President's National Security Strategy," Web page. n.d.

[2] In addition, in May 2006 the United States normalized relations with Libya in response to that country's changed behavior on terrorism and weapons of mass destruction. As recently as March 2006 the Department of State still characterized Libya as an authoritarian regime that practiced torture and systematically abridged civil rights. U.S. Department of State, "Libya: Country Reports on Human Rights Practices, 2005," Web page, March 8, 2006.

[3] In an interview for this report, one high-ranking official at the Department of State even challenged the assumption that the United States was engaged in a "war of ideas." The official's views are not important on the merits of the argument, only that clear and consistent rhetoric delivered by the President and Secretary of State does not ensure support from some sectors of the bureaucracy in translating policy statements into actions.

U.S. Government Programs and Challenges for the Future

This report is focused on building networks of moderate and liberal Muslims, but the dilemma outlined above highlights the fact that the U.S. government, and other Western governments, for that matter, does not have a consistent view on who the moderates are, where the opportunities for building networks among them lie, and how best to build the networks. As there is no clear and universally understood strategy, the U.S. engagement in the "war of ideas" is pursued most frequently in a compartmentalized fashion, focusing on agency- and country-specific efforts; it has been devised along traditional programmatic lines: democratization and governance; civil society; economic development; education and cultural exchanges; and women's empowerment. In many of these areas the United States is attempting to identify existing moderate individuals and organizations and provide them with financial, political, and technical support. However, network building among these disparate components is rarely an explicit goal. As a result, in spite of their good intentions, few of these efforts yield objective measures of success that allow for strategic budgeting of financial, human, and political capital.

Consequently, the United States exposes itself to three risks, all of which pose obstacles to successful network building: (1) misdirection, (2) wasted effort through duplication, and (3) missed opportunities. In the first case, the United States may work through programs or interlocutors who lack the credibility needed to champion liberal values or who may in fact oppose them, for example the Islamist *Parti de Justice et Développement* [Party of Justice and Development] (PJD) in Morocco or the Jordanian Muslim Brotherhood (also known as the Islamic Action Front).[4] In the second case, different agencies, and even offices within the same agency, may expend resources in pursuit of the same objective. Without adequate communication and command and control within the U.S. government, efforts may overlap, causing unnecessary opportunity costs. Lastly, because the process of choosing

---

[4]   See Jeremy M. Sharp, *U.S. Democracy Promotion Policy in the Middle East: The Islamist Dilemma*, Congressional Research Service report (RL33486), June 15, 2006, pp. 14–17, 27.

and supporting partners exposes both the United States and its part-ners to some level of risk, the natural degree of risk aversion in gov-ernment bureaucracies may inhibit active support for moderates and reformers, exacerbating the sense of isolation felt by moderates lacking self-sustaining support structures.

For analytical purposes, moderate network building can be said to proceed at three levels: (1) bolstering existing networks, (2) identify-ing potential networks and promoting their inception and growth, and (3) fostering an underlying condition of pluralism and tolerance that would prove more favorable to the growth of these networks. Although there are a number of U.S. government programs that are having posi-tive effects at the first two levels, most U.S. efforts to date fall within the third level, since programs aimed at ameliorating general condi-tions are more consistent with bureaucratic cultures—they can be more easily adapted to standard operating procedures and pose a lower level of risk.

The use of traditional public diplomacy to communicate and clarify U.S. policy, for instance, has been a staple of Department of State (and earlier USIA) activities over the last several decades; it is the approach with which the agency is most comfortable. In addition to individual or organizational preferences for programs that fall in the third level, as noted earlier, in many parts of the Muslim world there are few existing moderate networks or organizations with which the United States could partner. Unfortunately, in identifying oppor-tunities to promote the formation of moderate networks, the United States must contend with repressive environments and high levels of anti-Americanism.[5]

Democracy Promotion

The number of democratic states in the international system has increased dramatically over the last century, although the Middle East

---

[5]   Because this report made no efforts to explore clandestine U.S. programs, we cannot draw any conclusions about the scope or nature of any such programs.

still suffers from a "democracy deficit." Within the policy community, there seems to be a consensus that working to ensure free and fair elections is a necessary, but insufficient, step toward building democracy; freedom of speech, religion, assembly, and petition all require the establishment of self-sustaining institutions built on the rule of law, the protection of minority and gender rights, and transparency in government. Recently, however, there has been a "backlash" against democracy promotion from both illiberal regimes and publics that share, albeit for different reasons, a combination of fear and resentment towards external influence.[6]

Difficult even in the most welcoming climate, democracy-promotion efforts, especially in the Middle East, frequently clash with regimes that fear democracy as a threat to their political interests and actively resist it through laws prohibiting the establishment of opposition political parties or intimidation of pro-democracy NGO activity.[7] Democracy-promotion efforts are also confronted by resistance from other groups, most notably radical Islamists. Domestically, a tight federal budget and violent resistance to U.S. democracy-promotion efforts in Iraq and Afghanistan have led to waning support among Congress and the American public for what many consider to be too difficult a task with too little to show in the way of tangible results. In addition, because the liberal process of democratization can lead to illiberal electoral results, most notably in the recent victory of *Harakat al-Muqawama al-Islamiyya* [the Islamic Resistance Movement] (HAMAS) in the Palestinian Territories, there is increasing wariness about pressing secular authoritarians to open their political systems if there is a risk that radical Islamists will take their place.

---

[6] National Endowment for Democracy, *The Backlash Against Democracy Assistance: A Report Prepared by the National Endowment for Democracy for Senator Richard G. Lugar, Chairman, Committee on Foreign Relations, United States Senate*, Washington, D.C.: National Endowment for Democracy, June 8, 2006.

[7] In *The Backlash Against Democracy Assistance* (National Endowment for Democracy, 2006), Libya, Saudi Arabia, Sudan, Syria, and Uzbekistan are listed as "effectively prohibiting" democracy assistance efforts and independent NGOs, with Bahrain, Egypt, and Tunisia as "severely restricting them" and Jordan and Morocco as "largely tolerat[ing] but subject[ing] them] to arbitrary interference and/or harassment."

Amidst these systemic challenges, the United States is engaging in a number of efforts, both directly and indirectly, to promote democracy. Through traditional diplomatic channels, the United States is engaging in state-to-state dialogue and has crafted incentives (e.g., The Millennium Challenge Account) for states to join the "community of democracies." Publicly and privately, the United States emphasizes to its interlocutors and to the international community the benefits of adopting the liberal, democratic values of equity, tolerance, pluralism, the rule of law, and respect for civil and human rights. This emphasis on democratic values serves to contribute to the development of a political and social environment that facilitates the formation of moderate networks.

In addition, both the Department of State and USAID have specific democracy-promotion mandates, headed respectively by the Department of State's Bureau of Democracy, Human Rights, and Labor (DRL) and USAID's Bureau of Democracy, Conflict, and Humanitarian Assistance. In 2002, the Department of State launched MEPI, which contains a "political pillar" (see the MEPI case study below). DRL draws on considerable resources ($48 million for FY 2005) in the form of a "Human Rights and Democracy Fund" that is designed to promote "innovative, cutting-edge programs as a catalyst to improve human rights and promote democracy [with] projects that have an immediate, short-term impact." The USAID mandate includes "strengthening the performance and accountability of government institutions, combating corruption, and addressing the causes and consequences of conflict."[8]

To translate these policy goals into action, DRL and USAID contract with NGOs, principally the National Endowment for Democracy (NED), the International Republican Institute (IRI), the National Democratic Institute (NDI), the Asia Foundation, and the recently

---

[8]   Scott Tarnoff and Larry Nowels, *Foreign Aid: An Introductory Overview of U.S. Programs and Policy*, Congressional Research Service report (98-916), April, 15, 2004.

established Center for the Study of Islam and Democracy (CSID), all private, nonprofit organizations funded by the U.S. government.[9]

It is at this implementation level that efforts to bolster existing networks and identify and promote new networks take place. The programs implemented by these contractors provide technical assistance and campaigning skills to political parties, train electoral commissions, provide election monitoring guidance and oversight, establish or strengthen anti-corruption institutions, and stage conferences and workshops that bring together groups of individuals with common political goals, such as lawyers and judges seeking to strengthen the rule of law. For example, IRI conducts training programs "to bring traditional leadership networks into the democratic process" in order to bolster existing networks.[10]

As an example of an explicit network-building effort, DRL and NDI co-sponsored a "Congress of Democrats from the Islamic World" for ministers, government officials, and political-party representatives to discuss issues such as "the role of a democratic rule of law in Islamic societies."[11] Together, these efforts serve to build moderate networks on all three levels: bolstering networks where political parties exist, identifying and promoting potential networks when like-minded individuals lack a focal point or organizational capacity to coalesce, and contributing to the underlying conditions of moderation through the inherently moderate substance of the programs.

Invariably, the work of these institutions is well respected among U.S. officials and analysts, as well as local activists. Though their operating budgets come from the U.S. government,[12] their activities main-

---

[9] The CSID proposes to develop networks of Muslim democrats, including Islamists who in the CSID view adhere to a democratic agenda, and is partially funded by DRL. The CSID approach to network building is controversial—some believe that CSID's inclusive approach is necessary, but others are critical of working with Islamists. One view in the Department of State (outside of DRL) is that State's funding of CSID is an "experiment."

[10] International Republican Institute, "Partners in Peace," Web page, n.d.

[11] National Democratic Institute, "Congress of Democrats from the Islamic World," *The Middle East and North Africa in Focus: Regional Initiatives,* [June 2004].

[12] The operating budget of the Asia Foundation relies only partly on U.S. government funding, as is noted elsewhere.

tain a higher degree of credibility among recipient communities than if the programs were promoted directly by U.S. government agencies; it is accepted that their mission is assisting local forces of reform, not imposing it from the outside. Just one or two degrees of separation enable these contractors to provide network-building assistance without the perception of geopolitical strings attached. Most analysts suggest that the work of these nonpartisan, nongovernment agencies is the most effective means by which the United States can support democratic values. There is wide agreement that the Asia Foundation—the most successful of these NGOs in civil-society building—needs a replication tailored to the Middle East.

Nonetheless, while consistent with the policy goal of spreading democracy, these efforts are difficult to subject to outcome-based performance measures. Traditionally, the importance of such efforts has been measured by inputs (budgets, the number of countries hosting programs, the number of programs, etc.), while their effectiveness has been tracked by the outputs most easily observed (the number of training sessions held, the number of election monitors in place, attendance at conferences, etc.). But these observable data points do not necessarily translate into "democracy" per se, especially considering how many other variables can help or impede democratic progress.

There are some tangible measures of whether democratic values and institutions are gaining strength, such as voter turnout, the number of women and minority candidates competing for and winning elected office, and the freedom to campaign and engage in open political debate. It is harder, however, to link democratization programs to these outcomes in a clearly causal relationship. Moreover, the road to democracy is often long and indirect, so that even if such programs are effective in promoting democracy, the "proof" may not appear for several years, or even decades.

Lastly, because democratization programs come frequently through USAID contractors, the scope of traditional mechanisms for promoting democracy in wealthier countries such as Kuwait or Saudi

Arabia that receive no U.S. foreign aid is limited.[13] Because of the limited reach of legacy democratization programs in these countries, initiatives such as MEPI were in part designed to help fill in the gap by circumventing host-government involvement and by fostering regional-level programs.

Attempts to build moderate networks at all three levels should proceed in spite of the difficulty of measuring democratic outcomes; as the Cold War example demonstrated, moderate networks need not wait for democracy to bloom. The very process of promoting democracy inherently involves precisely the type of network building this project recommends. It is worth noting, however, that such network building, while certainly supportive of moderates, may also unintentionally provide financial and technical support to Islamists or their advocates who seek to gain power through democratic mechanisms, particularly if the vetting process is not sufficiently sensitive to the typology of Islam provided elsewhere in this report.

Civil-Society Development

The promotion of democracy goes forward hand in hand with the development of civil society; in fact, many in academia and the policy world consider civil society a necessary precursor to democracy. Civil society refers broadly to a set of institutions and values that serves as both a buffer and a critical link between the state and individuals; it is manifested when voluntary civic and social organizations (such as NGOs) can stand in opposition to forces brought by the state.

While civil society develops most easily in democracies, its development is both possible and desirable in non- and pre-democratic states. In fact, in these states civil-society development and network building are integrally linked; they are both mutually reinforcing and mutually dependent.

---

[13] Interview with Ambassador Kurtzer, Woodrow Wilson School, Princeton, N.J., May 22, 2006.

In theory, as civil society emerges, moderate networks follow, and vice versa. In practice, U.S. efforts at civil-society development are even broader than democracy promotion—they include all of the programs designed for democracy promotion plus those with mandates not so squarely involved with democracy per se. These include programs promoting economic opportunity, independent and responsible media, environmental protection, protection of minority or gender rights, and access to health care and education. For some, civil-society development provides an indirect approach to political reform—it fosters the skills and institutions needed in a functioning liberal democracy while minimizing the direct challenge to ruling regimes. This approach takes a long view, building democracy and liberal values through a grass-roots, bottom-up effort that poses specific challenges to U.S. government agencies, particularly the Department of State, which traditionally has focused on engaging with governments.

As with democracy promotion, U.S. policies on civil-society development are designed and overseen primarily by the Department of State and USAID, which in turn rely on contractors for implementation. For example, NED gives grants both to support existing local NGOs (for example, to help the Algerian League for the Defense of Human Rights promote awareness of the rule of law and respect for human rights) and to help promote the development of networks (for example, to help the Jordanian Center for Civic Education Studies develop the ability of Jordanian youth to engage civically through training of university students). NDI and IRI work as both contractors to USAID and subcontractors for NED. For example, IRI and NDI run Partners in Participation regional campaign schools in Qatar and Tunisia to increase the capacity of women to engage in civic affairs and to "facilitate ongoing networking between woman leaders in the region."[14]

The Asia Foundation, while focusing on similar projects, does not work exclusively as a contractor to the U.S. government, but rather draws funding from "a combination of private corporations and foundations, funding from governmental and multinational development

---

[14] International Republican Institute, "Partners in Peace," Web page, n.d.

agencies, and an annual appropriation from the U.S. Congress."[15] More so than NED, NDI, or IRI, the Asia Foundation explicitly seeks to build moderate Muslim networks. Programs such as the Institute for the Study of Islam and Society in Indonesia, which provides tolerance training for mosque youth leaders,[16] and the Islamic Foundation Bangladesh, which seeks to bring religious leaders to engage in human rights, public health, environmental conservation, and other issues,[17] are designed to work at all three levels of network building. Consequently, the Asia Foundation model is lauded by a great number of regional and functional experts. There is wide and deep support for the establishment of a Middle East Foundation that replicates the structure of the Asia Foundation, tailoring its approach to the culture and social and political environment of the Middle East. As of the drafting of this report, it appears that the U.S. government is putting this vision into reality with the Broader Middle East and North Africa (BMENA) Foundation for the Future, discussed in greater detail below.

Like democracy promotion, U.S. policies toward building civil society operate on all three levels of moderate network building: strengthening existing organizations, promoting new ones, and contributing to an environment of moderation that facilitates more focused efforts at the first two levels. Because civil society itself is based on transparency, dialogue, toleration, and peaceful political advocacy, it can be seen properly as a direct counterweight to extremism and violence. Moreover, because civil society emphasizes values over specific political outcomes, its development offers a method of engaging in political reform from the outside with a greatly reduced risk of resistance from intended recipients. For example, conferences on the promotion and protection of freedom of speech reflect widely shared yearnings that span geographic, linguistic, and cultural boundaries. Educational reform efforts, scholarships, and student and cultural exchanges all enjoy high degrees of demand and support among policymakers and analysts in part because they are so well received abroad. Similarly,

---

[15] The Asia Foundation, "The Asia Foundation: Overview," Web page, n.d.

[16] The Asia Foundation, "The Asia Foundation: Indonesia, Projects," Web page, n.d.

[17] The Asia Foundation, "The Asia Foundation: Bangladesh, Projects," Web page, n.d.

workshops on the establishment of independent and responsible media resonate with a variety of publics accustomed to state control of the marketplace of ideas.

In cases in which the NGOs and networks already exist, even minimal levels of financial, organizational, and technical support can prove crucial to ensuring their longevity and growth. Where no organizations or networks currently function, the convening of like-minded individuals and groups can move them to a critical "tipping point" of mutual awareness and support, as in the case of the USAID-supported Arab Civitas network of schools and educators supportive of moderate values that might otherwise struggle without the mutual support of sympathetic educators. Because civil society has traditionally been so lacking in the Middle East, the very concept of non-state institutions needs bolstering, both in theory and in practice. Notably, in at least one case the United States has begun to break free from traditional state-to-state aid delivery: The Brownback Amendment to the FY 2005 Consolidated Appropriations Act (P.L. 108-447) empowered U.S. agencies such as USAID to approach and support Egyptian NGOs without having to seek prior approval from the Egyptian government.

Despite its potential advantages, civil-society building faces two primary obstacles: active resistance by authoritarian regimes and a lack of tangible performance measurement criteria. Although authoritarian regimes might not consider all civil-society building initiatives as threats to their power (for example, the promotion of student associations), the very nature of civil society represents a challenge to state monopoly over the public sphere and a barrier to state authority over otherwise private realms. This resistance is manifested in laws prohibiting NGOs from forming or from accepting external support, strict monitoring of NGO activity, and, more recently, direct action against international NGOs (for example, the expulsion of the NDI Program Director from Bahrain[18] and the suspension of IRI activities by the Egyptian government[19]). In addition, civil-society building is beset by some of the same performance measurement problems as democracy

---

[18] William T. Monroe, "NDI's Positive Role Highlighted," interview, May 13, 2006.

[19] Sharp, 2006.

promotion, perhaps even more so, since there are no outputs that translate well into a representation of the strength of civil society.[20]

Considering these challenges, some see the proper focus of U.S. efforts to be the provision of tangible social services and other public goods, as these offer more direct manifestations of how the United States can improve people's lives. Those holding this view consider civil-society development to be confined to relatively small circles of elites (1) that aim to satisfy the needs of grant makers and not the societies these individuals represent[21] and (2) whose liberal values do not translate well into combating the more prosaic efforts of extremists, such as hospitals, schools, and jobs programs run by groups such as HAMAS and Hezbollah. One idea, put forth by analysts such as Dennis Ross, is for the United States to identify committed reformers to initiate a "secular *da'wa*," by which forces of moderation would be associated with tangible improvements in living conditions. This concept was endorsed throughout the Cold War through the establishment of agencies such as USAID and the Peace Corps.[22]

---

[20] Many NGOs have very brief operating spans, often with the same individuals forming, folding, and re-forming organizations under different names. In addition, the number of NGOs does not necessarily correlate to their power to provide a buffer between the private and official state spheres. Still, indicators such as increasing numbers of independent media outlets in operation, petitions filed, peaceful protests conducted, community health or conservation projects launched, and alternative educational curricula all suggest the development of civil society in the Middle East. With regard to network building, although a number of projects involve explicit or implicit aims on one or more of the three levels outlined above, we have uncovered no systematic attempt to track the quantity or quality of the resultant networks. As with democracy promotion, consistent performance criteria with definitive impact on civil society are difficult to define, and efforts to solicit and evaluate grant proposals are not matched by sufficient long-term follow-up monitoring and evaluation.

[21] Author's interview with Mona Yacoubian, United States Institute for Peace, June 7, 2006.

[22] Author's interview with Dennis Ross, Washington Institute for Near East Policy, May 26, 2006.

Public Diplomacy

Secretary of State Condoleezza Rice has engaged in an effort to encourage the Department of State and the broader U.S. government to pursue "transformational diplomacy," in which U.S government officials integrate public diplomacy into both policy design and implementation. But within the government, the objectives of public diplomacy remain varied. Some see its proper role as providing unbiased information, while others see it as a policy tool for influencing foreign audiences. Even when considered in the most positive light, public diplomacy is seen by many in Congress and at senior levels in the Bush administration as far less deserving of resources and strategic planning than the "harder" aspects of the war on terrorism, yet still more deserving than democracy-promotion or civil-society programs.[23]

Because it is designed primarily to support U.S. goals, or at least a more objective understanding of them, public diplomacy's ability to affect network-building efforts is confined almost exclusively to improving the underlying conditions within the Muslim world.[24] Not surprisingly, its effects in this arena are diffuse and hard to measure. Attendance at talks by U.S. officials, audiences of U.S.-sponsored radio and television broadcasts, and circulation of literature can be measured, as can trends in beliefs, moods, perceptions, and attitudes of target audiences (using polling and surveys such as those conducted by the Department of State's Bureau of Intelligence and Research). It

---

[23] A number of reports have been conducted with the aim of diagnosing the shortcomings of U.S. public diplomacy policy and prescribing methods of improving it. See U.S. Government Accountability Office, *U.S. Public Diplomacy: State Department Efforts to Engage Muslim Audiences Lack Certain Communications Elements and Face Persistent Challenges*, GAO-06-535, Washington, D.C.: May 3, 2006; Office of the Undersecretary of Defense for Acquisition, Technology, and Logistics, *Report of the Defense Science Board Task Force on Strategic Communications* , September 2004; and Advisory Group on Public Diplomacy for the Arab and Muslim World, *Changing Minds, Winning Peace: A New Strategic Direction for U.S. Public Diplomacy in the Arab & Muslim World: Report of the Advisory Group on Public Diplomacy for the Arab and Muslim World, Submitted to the Committee on Appropriations, U.S. House of Representatives*, October 1, 2003.

[24] Though, as the Radio Free Europe example instructs, there are opportunities for promoting new networks.

is far more difficult, however, to establish definitive links between the content of the programs and any measured changes in beliefs, moods, and perceptions. In addition, there is a general consensus among both U.S. officials and outside analysts that public diplomacy still suffers from secondary-status treatment within the Department of State and, particularly with regard to the Muslim world, from a deficit of language skills and historical and cultural knowledge within the U.S. government.

The high-profile appointment of Karen Hughes as the Undersecretary of State for Public Diplomacy signaled the Bush administration's intention to reinvigorate public diplomacy in the Muslim world. Unlike previous holders of this post, Hughes was known as an influential advisor to the President. In an April 2006 NSC memorandum, Hughes was designated chair of a Policy Coordination Committee on Public Diplomacy and Strategic Communication, a senior-level interagency group formed to conduct country-specific plans, including the identification of religious and cultural "key influencers."[25] One of the more tangible symbols of the new approach is reflected in the establishment of the Rapid Reaction Unit (RRU) in the Department of State's Bureau of Public Affairs and the upcoming Media Hubs in Brussels and Dubai. The RRU has a mandate to monitor Arabic broadcast and online media, providing daily excerpts along with analytical context and guidance for response. Operational only a few months after its conception, the RRU has had positive feedback from cabinet-level officials. Contrary to departmental standard operating procedure, the RRU does not subject its written products to other Department of State bureaus for clearance.

Others have expressed concern at the lack of support for public diplomacy from Congress and traditionalists in the Foreign Service. Within the Department of State, there is a lack of consensus on whether public diplomacy should be aimed at changing opinion, garnering support for policy, or isolating and marginalizing extremists. This strategic uncertainty ensures suboptimal policy performance. As one senior foreign service officer commented, "If this 'war of ideas' is a huge issue,

---

[25] Government Accountability Office, 2006.

why are we tinkering? . . . We as a government need to resolve the question of 'what is important.' If the war of ideas is not, let's stop pretending, because otherwise we can make it worse by exacerbating the problem of rhetoric outpacing action with tangible results."[26]

The mechanisms to deliver public diplomacy in the Muslim world have been dominated by radio and satellite television broadcasting. The FY 2007 funding request for the Broadcasting Board of Governors (BBG), which includes both Radio Sawa and the U.S. Middle East Television Network (Al Hurra), was $671.9 million plus an emergency supplemental of $50 million for broadcasting into Iran,[27] together representing ten times the total budget of MEPI. While one analyst declared Al Hurra "a total disaster" for its inability to gain market share,[28] Radio Sawa has been fairly successful in building an audience. Success in building an audience, however, does not clearly result in net gains in general moderation or more tangible forms of network building. Typifying the negativity surrounding Al Hurra, an analyst intimately involved with the station decried the fact that almost no senior administration officials have appeared for on-camera interviews on the network in the last year.[29] It is far from clear that either Radio Sawa or Al Hurra has positively shaped attitudes toward U.S. policies, and the large operating budgets devoted to maintaining these programs of dubious value draw resentment from those in the U.S. government and the larger policy community who see them as imposing disproportionate opportunity costs.

In order to better match foreign-policy goals with programs, resources, and bureaucratic responsibilities, the Secretary of State

---

[26] Author's interview with Alberto Fernandez, Department of State, Bureau of Near Eastern Affairs, June 7, 2006.

[27] Larry Nowels, Connie Veillette, Susan B. Epstein, *Foreign Operations (House)/State, Foreign Operations, and Related Programs (Senate): FY2007 Appropriations,* Congressional Research Service report (RL33420), May 25, 2006.

[28] Author's interview with Steven Cook, Council on Foreign Relations, June 9, 2006. Mr. Cook also commented that "proper blame [for Al Hurra] is shared between the Administration for suggesting it and the Hill for agreeing to support it so generously."

[29] Author's interview with Robert Satloff, Washington Institute for Near East Policy, June 26, 2006.

established the position of Director of Foreign Assistance in early 2006. Currently held by USAID Administrator Ambassador Randall L. Tobias, this position reflects the need to coordinate multiple offices that are pursuing a range of goals across qualitatively different political environments, as depicted graphically in the Department of State's Foreign Assistance Framework.[30]

Time will tell how this organizational change might improve the strategic use of limited resources, but there is little doubt that the new office will be challenged by a range of entrenched bureaucratic practices and interests, limited authority outside of USAID and Department of State activities, and, at a more fundamental level, the lack of clear and consistent political criteria for qualifying recipients of assistance.[31]

Case Study: The Middle East Partnership Initiative

Although it is far from the largest U.S. program of engagement with the Muslim world, MEPI represents a high-profile attempt to break free from pre-9/11 standard approaches by structuring its programs on four thematic "pillars"—politics, economics, education, and women's empowerment—and by supporting indigenous NGOs directly on a more innovative and flexible basis. Initiated in December 2002 by then–Secretary of State Colin Powell, the MEPI structure appears to be a response to the self-perceived shortfalls of the Arab world as outlined in the United Nations Development Programme (UNDP) *Arab Human Development Report 2002*.[32] As a new office in the Bureau of Near Eastern Affairs (NEA), MEPI is designed to veer away from the Department of State's conventional government-to-government approach and to rely on U.S.-based NGOs as implementation contrac-

---

[30] Reproduced in Appendix A.

[31] See Larry Nowels and Connie Veillette, *Restructuring U.S. Foreign Aid: The Role of the Director of Foreign Assistance*, Congressional Research Service report (RS22411), September 8, 2006.

[32] United Nations Development Programme, *Arab Human Development Report 2002: Creating Opportunities for Future Generations*, New York: United Nations Development Programme, 2002.

tors. These NGOs disburse funds received from MEPI as small grants directly to indigenous NGOs operating within the framework of the four "pillars."[33]

MEPI's adoption of this "venture-capital" approach gives it greater flexibility and willingness to accept risk in promoting its agenda than more established bureaucratic entities. However, the organization has been criticized (for instance, in an August 2005 Government Accountability Office [GAO] report)[34] for lacking performance measurements and evaluation criteria. Over the last few years, however, MEPI has instituted extensive screening procedures and has retained Management Systems International, which has experience working with USAID, to assist with evaluation criteria and program monitoring. As of the drafting of this report, these criteria were still in development. MEPI's own list of success stories includes a number of indicators of inputs and outputs, but the organization lacks a clear link between these indicators and evidence of reform outcomes. For example, in contrast to the voter intimidation and repression of opposition candidates in the recent elections in Egypt seen by some democratization analysts as a lack of progress, MEPI lists as one of its success stories its support for 2,000 domestic election monitors observing that election.[35]

In terms of network building, MEPI programs operate at all three levels and across the four "pillars." In the political pillar, MEPI programs have included explicit attempts to form networks of legal reform experts in the "Middle East Associate Rights Initiative" and of civil-society promoters in the Al-Urdun Al-Jadid Research Center (an initiative to convene reformers interested in constitutional and electoral politics, media, and women and youth); the Civic Democratic Initiatives Support Foundation (which aims to establish national and

---

[33] The same four headings were contained in the UNDP's *Arab Human Development Report, 2002.*

[34] U.S. Government Accountability Office, *Foreign Assistance: Middle East Partnership Initiative Offers Tools for Supporting Reform, but Project Monitoring Needs Improvement*, GAO-05-700, August 2005.

[35] For more examples, see Middle East Partnership Initiative, "Success Stories," Web page, n.d.

regional NGO networks); and the Egyptian Association for Supporting Democracy (which provides leadership and skills training to trade and student unions and youth clubs, among others).

In the economic pillar, MEPI's network-building activities include connecting investment policymakers from the region with those from member countries of the Organisation for Economic Co-Operation and Development (OECD), strengthening Moroccan agricultural associations, and conducting policy workshops for customs and trade officials.

Within the education pillar, MEPI supports the efforts of Arab Civitas to promote civic-education programs that link students and educators throughout the region; a program in Morocco that convenes administrators, educators, school supporters, and advisory councils to improve the quality and access to primary education, especially for girls; and a number of networking activities that link American educational communities with their counterparts in the region.

MEPI programs in the women's empowerment pillar include support for the Arab Women's Legal Network; a program in Egypt to strengthen women's NGO networks; and a number of technical training and advocacy workshops aimed at improving women's educational, economic, and social conditions.

Generally, aside from Congress, MEPI has enjoyed widespread support in the policy community for moving the U.S. government in the right direction, although it remains exposed to a number of criticisms regarding its ability to carry out its stated goals. First and foremost, those who support the MEPI approach lament its lack of financial and political capital and its weak hand in departmental and inter-agency battles over authority and budget. Second, while MEPI is lauded for filling a niche left vacant by traditional development and democratization programs run by DRL and USAID, critics have claimed that MEPI's contractors include many of the "usual suspects" among American and international NGOs. For instance, early critics pointed out that because MEPI grant applications are offered exclusively in English, most of the potential local NGO recipients are excluded from applying; MEPI is now offering application materials in Arabic and French and mandating that MEPI field-office personnel identify and encourage applications from nontraditional recipients and offer assistance in translating concept papers into full-fledged grant proposals. Third, the venture-capital model exposes MEPI to the accusation that its programs are ad hoc and motivated more by public relations than achieving results. While MEPI continues to accept a degree of risk by supporting heretofore untested entities, it has put procedures in place to guard against opportunism, both before and after approving grant applications.

MEPI's strengths (agility, novelty, regional approach, and risk acceptance) have caused institutional difficulties. As MEPI is the newest member of the Freedom Agenda team and moves beyond traditional country-specific programmatic approaches to regional initiatives, it lacks champions on the Hill and encounters institutional resistance within the Department of State. MEPI activities span the jurisdictions of multiple authorizing committees, and MEPI is not earmarked in appropriations bills, presenting perhaps an easy target in an era of tightening budgets. Possibly for these reasons, MEPI funding levels have been dropping, with FY 2007 funding coming some $45 million below the administration's request of $120 million.[36]

Moreover, MEPI programs are often unpopular with local governments, and their displeasure constitutes an irritant for U.S. embassy officials, desk officers, and their superiors, all of whom naturally wish to avoid friction with host governments. MEPI has chosen not to renew some projects,[37] but it is not clear which ones or on what basis—insufficient funds, unsatisfactory progress, or a determination that continued funding would not be in the best interests of the United States.[38] The urgency with which MEPI hoped to identify and support indigenous

---

[36] U.S. Department of State, "FY 2007 International Affairs (Function 150) Budget Request," February 6, 2006.

[37] Author's interview with Tammy Wincup, MEPI Office Director, Bureau of Near Eastern Affairs, Department of State, May 24, 2006.

[38] U.S. Government Accountability Office, *Foreign Assistance: Middle East Partnership Initiative Offers Tools for Supporting Reform but Project Monitoring Needs Improvement*, GAO-05-711, August 2005.

NGOs has often been stymied by a lack of operational capacity to deliver support in the form of grant disbursal or technical support.[39]

Lastly, while MEPI touts the potential rewards of engaging directly with moderates, its very inception was met with negative reactions by those who believed that the initiative had been launched without adequate consultation with local reformers or other parties also interested in promoting democracy and liberal reform.[40] From the beginning, MEPI has instituted a number of mechanisms to increase coordination, both within the Department of State and with its European Commission counterparts, including regular policy- and implementation-level meetings. In 2004, the United States, together with its G8 partners, attempted to inject a multilateral approach with the launching of the BMENA Initiative. Although the only tangible BMENA Initiative activities through June 2006 have been two summit conferences, it appears as if the initiative will respect some of the criticisms and recommendations offered by critics of MEPI and the larger U.S. effort.

The BMENA Foundation for the Future

In consulting experts from government, academia, and think tanks, the closest thing to a consensus on network building has emerged around the need to adopt an indirect, regional, multilateral approach that enables the United States to support the forces of moderation without falling prey to accusations of interference in domestic and Muslim affairs. Time and again, officials and analysts have voiced their hope that the model of the Asia Foundation will be replicated in and tailored to the Middle East region. In July 2006, this vision will be put in practice with the first scheduled meeting of the Board of Directors of the BMENA Foundation for the Future.

---

[39] For an example of the difficulties facing grant recipients, see Lindsay Wise, "Show Them the Money: Why Is an American Program Aimed at Supporting Reform in the Arab World Coming Under Attack by Its Own Beneficiaries?" *Cairo Magazine*, July 25, 2005.

[40] See, for example, Tamara Cofman Wittes, "The Promise of Arab Liberalism," *Policy Review*, July 2004; or Amy Hawthorne, "The Middle East Partnership Initiative: Questions Abound," *Arab Reform Bulletin*, Vol. 1, No. 3, September 2003.

An outgrowth of the G8's BMENA Initiative, the mission of the foundation is "to support civil society organizations in their efforts to foster democracy and freedom in the BMENA region"[41] with financial and political capital from the United States; European, Middle Eastern, and North African governments; and the European Union. As of June 2006, over $50 million had been committed, of which $35 million were from the United States and administered by MEPI. While the programs generated by $50 million will not produce immediate or systematic shifts toward moderation, they might prove sufficient to establish the model and to attract additional donations from states, multinational corporations, and philanthropic organizations and individuals.

The BMENA Foundation for the Future takes a studiously nonpolitical approach to reform, prohibiting active government officials from sitting on its board of directors and stating in its charter principles that it will not fund political parties. The foundation has three principal goals:

1. To create an indigenous mechanism to fulfill the commitment made in the many recent declarations on reform and democracy
2. To mobilize funds from inside and outside the region to assist indigenous initiatives for reform and democracy with international support
3. To bring together existing pro-democracy initiatives into a process that links national, regional, and international movements for democratization.

In addition, the foundation is focused explicitly and exclusively on building and strengthening indigenous capacity. Its charter principles stipulate a commitment to "providing financial and technical assistance to local non-governmental organizations, academic institutions, professional associations based in the region; and undertaking programs and activities that contribute to the strengthening of free-

---

[41] BMENA Foundation for the Future, "Mission and Mandate," Web page, n.d.

doms and democracy in the region."[42] If, in fact, the foundation is able to fulfill this vision, it will represent a significant diversion from traditional U.S. government approaches that seek local-government approval and rely heavily on U.S. and international NGOs for program implementation.

While it is far too early to judge the BMENA Foundation for the Future's prospects for success, it is notable that the United States is moving in the direction of building a multilateral, nongovernmental approach to strengthening democratic and civil-society institutions. For the U.S. government to support such an approach suggests that hopeful degrees of learning and adaptation have occurred over the course of the past five years.

Conclusions

Looking back over the past five years, the United States has faced a number of challenges in constructing a strategy for promoting democracy and freedom in the Middle East and broader Muslim world. Many of these challenges arise from domestic, local, and international factors beyond the control of the U.S. government.

Still, even with respect to those aspects that the United States can influence, there remain gaps in both strategic leadership and operational capacity. A consensus has yet to emerge on real and potential allies in the war of ideas, much less on the practices to follow—and avoid—in supporting them. Instead, most U.S. efforts thus far have seemed to follow familiar bureaucratic and programmatic standard operating procedures, with modifications with regard to the scope, rather than the type, of the efforts undertaken.

In addition, funding levels for the "soft-power" side of the war on terrorism continue to fall, while requested funding levels and appropriations for the military and other "hard-power" aspects continue to grow. For example, funding requests for FY 2007 included a 27.5 percent reduction in funding for the Asia Foundation ($10 million) and

---

[42] BMENA Foundation for the Future, "Mission and Mandate."

a flat request for NED ($80 million), reflecting the gap between the U.S. government's rhetorical stance on network building and its actual policy priorities.[43]

---

[43] Nowels et al., 2006.

CHAPTER FIVE

Road Map for Moderate Network Building in the Muslim World

Identifying Key Partners and Audiences

A critical part of U.S. network-building efforts, as well as in its broader public diplomacy and strategic communications policy, is identifying key partners and audiences. Difficulties in distinguishing potential allies from adversaries present a major problem to Western governments and organizations attempting to organize support for moderate Muslims. Work done by the RAND Corporation—in Cheryl Benard's *Civil Democratic Islam* and Angel Rabasa et al., *The Muslim World After 9/11*—has begun to lay the framework for identifying ideological tendencies in the Muslim world,[1] which is necessary in order to identify the sectors with which the United States and its allies can be most effective in promoting democracy and stability to counter the influence of extremist and violent groups.

Around the world Muslims differ substantially not only in their religious views, but also in their political and social orientation, including their conceptions of government; their views on the primacy of *shari'a* (Islamic law) versus other sources of law; their views on human rights, especially the rights of women and religious minorities; and whether they support, justify, or tolerate violence perpetrated

---

[1] Cheryl Benard, *Civil Democratic Islam,* Santa Monica: Calif.: RAND Corporation, MR-1716-CMEPP, 2003; and Angel M. Rabasa, Cheryl Benard, Peter Chalk, C. Christine Fair, Theodore Karasik, Rollie Lal, Ian Lesser, and David Thaler, *The Muslim World After 9/11,* Santa Monica, Calif.: The RAND Corporation, MG-246-AF, 2004.

in advancement of a political or religious agenda. We refer to these as "marker issues," and the position of groups or individuals on them allows for a more precise classification of these groups in terms of their affinity for democracy and pluralism.

Characteristics of Moderate Muslims

For purposes of this study, moderate Muslims are those who share the key dimensions of democratic culture. These include support for democracy and internationally recognized human rights (including gender equality and freedom of worship), respect for diversity, acceptance of nonsectarian sources of law, and opposition to terrorism and other illegitimate forms of violence.

Democracy

A commitment to democracy as understood in the liberal Western tradition and agreement that political legitimacy derives from the will of the people expressed through free and democratic elections is a key marker issue in identifying moderate Muslims. Some Muslims take the view common in the West that democratic values are universal and not contingent on particular cultural and religious contexts. Other moderate Muslims, however, take the view that democracy in the Muslim world has to be based on Islamic traditions and texts. They seek to contextualize these texts in ways that support democratic values and to find scriptural sources of democracy, as in the Quranic command that Muslims should order their collective affairs through consultation (shura). In either case, what matters is the results. Whether a political philosophy derives from Western or Quranic sources, to be considered democratic it must unequivocally support pluralism and internationally recognized human rights.

Support for democracy implies opposition to concepts of the Islamic state—particularly those that imply the exercise of political power by a self-appointed clerical elite, as in the case of Iran. Muslim moderates hold the view that no one can speak for God. Rather, it is the consensus of the community (ijma), as reflected in freely expressed public opinion, that determines what God's will is in any particular case. Within Twelver Shi'ite Islam there is a long tradition of quietism, a Shi'ite religious tradition that is wary of political authority, seeing it as lacking in divine sanction in the absence of the Imam. This tradition has been subverted by theocratic Khomeinist notions in Iran and in other places where the Iranian regime exercises influence; nevertheless, it persists in Iraq and elsewhere as a potential substratum for democratic development.[2]

Acceptance of Nonsectarian Sources of Law

The dividing line between moderate Muslims and radical Islamists in countries with legal systems based on those of the West (the majority of states in the Muslim world) is whether *shari'a* should apply. Conservative interpretations of *shari'a* are incompatible with democracy and internationally recognized human rights because, as noted liberal Sudanese intellectual Abdullahi An-Naim points out, men and women and believers and unbelievers do not have equal rights under *shari'a*. In addition, due to the diversities of opinion in Islamic law, any enactment of *shari'a* principles as law would mean enforcing the political will of those in power, selecting some opinions over others, and thereby denying believers and others freedom of choice.[3]

Respect for the Rights of Women and Religious Minorities

Moderates are hospitable to Muslim feminists and open to religious pluralism and interfaith dialogue. Moderates argue, for instance, that discriminatory injunctions in the Quran and the *sunna* relating to

---

[2] See Chapter 11, "The Modernity of Theocracy," in Juan Cole, *Sacred Space and Holy War: The Politics, Culture and History of Shi'ite Islam*, London and New York: I.B. Tauris, 2002. For the challenges of democracy promotion in the Middle East, see Thomas Carothers and Marina S. Ottaway, *Uncharted Journey: Promoting Democracy in the Middle East*, Washington, D.C.: Carnegie Endowment for International Peace, 2005; and Thomas Carothers, Marina S. Ottaway, Amy Hawthorne, and Daniel Brumberg, *Democratic Mirage in the Middle East*, Carnegie Policy Brief No. 20, Washington, D.C.: Carnegie Endowment for International Peace, October 2002.

[3] Abdullahi An-Naim, "Public Forum on Human Rights, Religion & Secularism," notes by Siew Foong on speech delivered by Abdullahi An-Naim, National Evangelical Christian Fellowship Malaysia, January 18, 2003.

women's position within the society and the family (for example, that a daughter's inheritance should be half that of a son's) should be reinterpreted on the grounds that conditions today are not the same as those that prevailed in the Prophet Muhammad's day. Moderates also defend women's right of access to education and health services and right to full participation in the political process, including the right to hold political offices. Similarly, moderates advocate equal citizenship and legal rights for non-Muslims.

Opposition to Terrorism and Illegitimate Violence

Moderate Muslims, just like adherents of other religious traditions, have a concept of the just war. According to Mansur Escudero, leader of the *Federación Española de Entidades Religiosas Islámicas* [Spanish Federation of Islamic Religious Entities] (FEERI), it would be false to say that Islam does not contemplate violence. The important thing is to define the ethical principles that regulate violence: what kinds of violence are legitimate and what kinds are not? How and in what form is violence employed is of outmost importance in determining its legitimacy. Violence against civilians and suicide operations, that is to say, terrorism, is not legitimate.[4] It is, however, legitimate to use violence defensively to protect Muslims against aggressors. Legitimate violence must respect normative limits, such as using the minimum force required, respecting the lives of noncombatants, and avoiding ambushes and assassinations.[5]

Application of Criteria

It follows from the above that for a group to declare itself "democratic" in the sense of favoring elections as the vehicle for establishing govern-

---

[4]   Author's discussion with Mansur Escudero, Spain, August 2005.

[5]   Patricia Martinez, "Deconstructing Jihad: Southeast Asian Contexts," in Kumar Ramakrishna and See Seng Tan, eds., *After Bali: The Threat of Terrorism in Southeast Asia*, Singapore: Institute of Defence and Strategic Studies, Nanyang Technological University, 2003; and Youssef Aboul-Enein and Sherifa Zuhur, *Islamic Rulings on Warfare*, Carlisle, Pa.: Strategic Studies Institute, U.S. Army War College, October 2004.

ment—as in the case of the present Egyptian Muslim Brotherhood—is not enough. Just as important is respect for freedom of expression, association, and religion (and the freedom *not* to be religious as well): what we called in *The Muslim World After 9/11* the "infrastructure of democratic political processes."[6] Therefore, in determining whether a group or movement meets this characterization of moderation, a reasonably complete picture of its worldview is needed. This picture can emerge from the answers given to the following questions:

- Does the group (or individual) support or condone violence? If it does not support or condone violence now, has it supported or condoned it in the past?
- Does it support democracy? And if so, does it define democracy broadly in terms of individual rights?
- Does it support internationally recognized human rights?
- Does it make any exceptions (e.g., regarding freedom of religion)?
- Does it believe that changing religions is an individual right?
- Does it believe the state should enforce the criminal-law component of *shari'a?*
- Does it believe the state should enforce the civil-law component of *shari'a?* Or does it believe there should be non-*shari'a* options for those who prefer civil-law matters to be adjudicated under a secular legal system?
- Does it believe that members of religious minorities should be entitled to the same rights as Muslims?
- Does it believe that a member of a religious minority could hold high political office in a Muslim majority country?
- Does it believe that members of religious minorities are entitled to build and run institutions of their faith (churches and synagogues) in Muslim majority countries?
- Does it accept a legal system based on nonsectarian legal principles?

---

[6] Rabasa et al., 2004, p. 6.

Beyond ideology, it is also necessary to ask questions about the relationships of these groups to other political actors and the consequences and effects of these relationships. For instance, are they aligned in political fronts with radical groups? Do they receive funding or support radical foundations?

Potential Partners

In general, there appears to be three broad sectors within the spectrum of ideological tendencies in the Muslim world where the United States and the West can find partners in the effort to combat Islamist extremism: secularists; liberal Muslims; and moderate traditionalists, including Sufis.

Secularists

Secularism in its various guises was the dominant conceptualization of the state's relationship with religion among political elites during the formative years of most modern Muslim states. However, in recent years secularism has steadily lost ground, partly because of the Islamic resurgence of the last three decades throughout large parts of the Muslim world, and partly because—especially in the Arab world—secularism has become associated not with Western models of liberal democracy, but with failed authoritarian political systems. Therefore, in promoting secular alternatives to Islamism, it is important to make some distinctions. Secularists in the Muslim world fall into three categories: liberal secularists, "anti-clericalists," and authoritarian secularists.

Liberal secularists support secular law and institutions within the context of a democratic society. They hold liberal or social-democratic values that form the core of a Western-style "civil religion." They believe in the separation of the political and religious spheres, but are not hostile to religion per se or to public manifestations of religion. The values of liberal secularists are closest in orientation to Western political values, but this group is a minority in the Muslim world. Nevertheless, our study of Muslim secularists has shown that, contrary to what is generally assumed, they are not a new or negligible phenomenon in the Muslim world (see Chapter Nine).

There is another school of secularism that is closer to the Ataturkist viewpoint and to the French tradition of *laiceté*. For lack of a better term, we refer to this category as "anti-clericalists" (although Sunni Islam does not have a clergy). In this tradition—which, although weakening, is still dominant in Turkey—the state is aggressively secular and open displays of religious identity are prohibited in schools or other official spaces. The battles over the wearing of *jihab*, the female Islamic head covering, in countries such as France, Tunisia, Turkey, and Singapore, are manifestations of the clash between the *état laique* and assertive manifestations of religiosity.

A third category of secularism is made up of authoritarian secularists; it includes Ba'athists, Nasserites, neo-Communists, and adherents of various other strains of authoritarianism. Although theoretically hostile to Islamism, authoritarian secularist leaders sometimes attempt to manipulate Islamic symbols and themes when politically expedient, as in the case of Saddam Hussein in his last years in power, and have been known to collaborate with Islamists against democratic reformers. Obviously, individuals and groups in this category would not be appropriate partners for the United States and Western democrats.

Liberal Muslims

Liberal Muslims differ from secularists in that their political ideology has a religious substratum—analogous to the European Christian Democrats—but they advocate an agenda that is compatible with Western notions of democracy and pluralism. Liberal Muslims may come from different Muslim traditions. They may be modernists, seeking to bring the core values of Islam into harmony with the modern world or, as in the case of the Indonesian liberal Muslim activist Ulil Abshar Abdallah and his Liberal Muslim Network, they might come from a traditionalist background.

What liberal Muslims have in common is a belief that Islamic values are consistent with democracy, pluralism, human rights, and individual freedoms, as indicated in this self-definition of liberal Islam:

The name of "Liberal Islam" illustrate[s] our fundamental principles; Islam which emphasizes on "private liberties" (according to
Mu'tazilah's doctrine regarding "human liberties"), and "liberation" of socio-political structure from the unhealthy and oppress-
ing domination. The "liberal" adjective has two meanings: "liberty" (being liberal) and "liberating." Please note that we do not
believe in Islam as such—Islam without any adjective as some
people argued. Islam is impossible without adjective, in fact Islam
[has] been interpreted in so many different ways in accordance to
the interpreter's need. We choose a genre of interpretation, and by
this way, we selected an adjective for Islam, it is "liberal."[7]

Liberal Muslims are hostile to the concept of the "Islamic state."
As noted Indonesian modernist and former Muhammadiyah chair-
man Ahmad Syafii Maarif points out, there is not a single verse in the
Quran on the organization of the state.[8]

Liberal Muslims discern the roots of Muslim democracy in the
Quranic concept of *shura*, which leads to their belief in an egalitarian
political system. In this view, an Islamic government must be democratic. It cannot be dynastic, which would be a grave deviation from
Islamic teachings, according to Syafii Maarif. In this sense, the Saudi
government is not Islamic, even if its constitution is the Quran.[9]

A consistent view in liberal modernist Muslim thinking is that
shari'a is a product of the historical circumstances of the time of its creation and that elements of it—for instance, corporal punishments—
are no longer contextual and therefore need to be modernized. In *Islam
and Liberty: The Historical Misunderstanding*, the noted Tunisian modernist thinker Mohammed Charfi argues that under Ummayad and
Abbasid rule Islamic law evolved in the context of an alliance between
theologians and politicians.[10] Although the law was dressed up as religion, it was written to suit the political needs of the rulers. At the time,

---

[7]   Liberal Islam Network, "About Liberal Islam Network," Web page, n.d.

[8]   Author's interview with Ahmad Syafii Maarif, Jakarta, June 2002.

[9]   Author's interview with Ahmad Syafii Maarif, Jakarta, May 2002.

[10]   Mohammed Charfi, *Islam and Liberty: The Historical Misunderstanding*, trans. Patrick
Camiller, New York: Zed Books, 2005.

the theory of the state was founded on authoritarianism, women were not equal under the law, and the legal system incorporated corporal punishments. These conditions existed everywhere else, Charfi argues, "but others evolved and we didn't."[11]

Moderate Traditionalists and Sufis

Traditionalists and Sufis probably constitute the large majority of Muslims. They are often, but not always, conservative Muslims who uphold beliefs and traditions passed down through the centuries—1,400 years of Islamic traditions and spirituality that are inimical to fundamentalist ideology, as stated by Abdurrahman Wahid.[12] These traditions incorporate the veneration of saints (and the offering of prayers at their tombs) and other practices that are anathema to the Wahhabis. They interpret the Islamic scriptures on the basis of the teachings of the schools of jurisprudence *(mazhab)* that were established in the early centuries of Islam; they do not engage in unmediated interpretation of the Quran and the *hadith* (the tradition of the Prophet Muhammad), as Salafists and modernists do. Many traditionalists incorporate elements of Sufism—the tradition of Islamic mysticism that stresses emotive and personal experiences of the divine—into their practice of Islam.

Immediately relevant to this study is the fact that Salafis and Wahhabis are relentless enemies of traditionalists and Sufis. Whenever radical Islamist movements have gained power they have sought to suppress the practice of traditionalist and Sufi Islam, as in the well-known destruction of early Islamic monuments in Saudi Arabia. Because of their victimization by Salafis and Wahhabis, traditionalists and Sufis are natural allies of the West to the extent that common ground can be found with them.

As we explore the possibility of partnerships with traditionalists and Sufis it is important to keep in mind the wide diversity of this

---

[11] Mohammed Charfi, conference, Hudson Institute, Washington, D.C., October 18, 2005.

[12] Abdurrahman Wahid, "Right Islam vs. Wrong Islam," *The Wall Street Journal*, December 30, 2005.

sector. In countries like Bosnia, Syria, Iran, Kazakhstan, and Indonesia, the Islam commonly practiced throughout local society is Sufi or Sufi-influenced but is a diffused phenomenon. In other countries, such as the Albanian lands, Morocco, Turkey, India, and Malaysia, Sufism exists in a disciplined, organized form.[13] Although in some cases Sufis have manifested radical tendencies and supported militant groups,[14] by and large Sufi groups fall on the moderate side of the divide. Some Sufi movements are militantly moderate; for instance, the *Jam'iyyat al-Mashari' al-Khayriyya al-Islamiyya Ahbash* [Society of Islamic Philanthropic Projects] of Lebanon emphasizes moderation and tolerance and opposes political activism and the use of violence.

The Turkish religious leader Fethullah Gulen promotes a form of moderate modern Sufi Islam. Gulen opposes the state's enforcement of Islamic law, pointing out that most Islamic regulations concern people's private lives and only a few bear on matters of governance. The state, he believes, should not enforce Islamic law: Because religion is a private matter, the requirements of any particular faith should not be imposed on an entire population. Gulen extends his ideas about tolerance and dialogue to Christians and Jews; he has twice met with Patriarch Bartholomeos, head of the Greek Orthodox Ecumenical Patriarchate in Istanbul, visited the Pope in Rome in 1998, and received a visiting chief rabbi from Israel.

Gulen asserts the compatibility of Islam and democracy and accepts the argument that the idea of republicanism is very much in accord with early Islamic concepts of *shura*. Gulen opposes any authoritarian regime that would impose strict controls on ideas and is very critical of the regimes in Iran and Saudi Arabia. He holds that the Turkish interpretation and experience of Islam are different from those of others, especially the Arabs. He writes of an "Anatolian Islam" that is based on tolerance and that excludes harsh restrictions or fanaticism.[15]

---

[13] Communication from Stephen Schwartz, July 25, 2006.

[14] Shmuel Bar, for instance, points out that the Muslim Brotherhood in Egypt and Syria was heavily Sufi. Author's discussion with Shmuel Bar, Washington, D.C., April 14, 2005.

[15] Bulent Aras and Omer Caha, "Fethullah Gulen and His Liberal 'Turkish Islam' Movement," *MERIA Journal*, Vol. 4, No. 4, December 2000. Gulen is regarded with suspicion by

Should Islamists Be Engaged?

Within the academic and policy communities in the United States and Europe there is a major debate surrounding the question of whether or not Islamists should be engaged as partners. Before outlining the two sides of the argument, we first need to define the term "Islamists." One definition is that they are simply Muslims with political agendas.[16] This definition is too broad to be useful, since it encompasses anyone involved in politics in the Muslim world. A narrower, more useful definition identifies Islamists as those who reject the separation of religious authority from the power of the state. Islamists seek to establish some version of an Islamic state, or at least the recognition of *shari'a* as the basis of law.[17]

The argument in favor of engaging Islamists has three attributes: first, that Islamists represent the only real mass-based alternative to authoritarian regimes in the Muslim world (and especially in the Arab world); second, that Islamist groups such as the Egyptian Muslim Brotherhood have evolved to support pluralistic democracy, women's rights, etc.;[18] and third, that Islamists are more likely to be successful in dissuading potential terrorists from committing violence than are mainstream clerics.[19]

Turkish secularists, who believe that he may be seeking to undermine the strict separation of religion and state under Turkey's Ataturkist constitution.

[16] Saad Eddin Ibrahim, presentation at Center for the Study of Islam and Democracy (CSID) Conference, Washington, D.C., April 22, 2005. Graham Fuller defines political Islam as the belief that the Quran and the *hadith* (the traditions of the Prophet Muhammad) have something important to say about how society and governance should be ordered. Graham Fuller, "The Future of Political Islam," *Foreign Affairs*, Vol. 81, No. 2, March/April 2002.

[17] This definition is given in Sue-Ann Lee, "Managing the Challenges of Radical Islam: Strategies to Win the Hearts and Minds of the Muslim World," seminar paper, John F. Kennedy School of Government, Harvard University, April 1, 2003.

[18] Ibrahim, 2005.

[19] This argument was made bluntly to one of the authors by a representative of a European foreign ministry.

According to Amr Hamzawy, in countries like Egypt there has been a convergence of left-leaning liberals and moderate Islamists on the rules of democracy, good governance, and anti-corruption. Hamzawy states that since the 1990s, the Muslim Brothers in Egypt have revisited their conception of politics and society. Their evolution includes a retreat from the goal of an Islamic state and a shift from conservative to less-conservative perceptions of society: for instance, a more modern view of women's rights. Hamzawy concedes that less-progressive zones do still exist within the Muslim Brotherhood. Moderate Islamists are not liberals. They harbor conservative views. Nevertheless, he believes that there is a window of opportunity for the United States to reach out to moderate Islamists, and that by engaging them the United States will be able to influence them.[20]

The U.S.-funded, Washington-based CSID subscribes to this approach. CSID aims to bring together scholars and activists to promote democracy in the Muslim world. The center's partners are secularists and moderate Islamists who believe in democracy and reject violence; the center engages these groups in discussions on conceptions of democracy, ways to implement it in their countries, areas of agreement and disagreement, and whether they can work together on the issues on which they agree.[21]

Some European governments are willing to recognize and promote Islamists, although in some cases this seems to stem more from an inability to distinguish Islamists from liberal Muslims than from a conscious policy. For instance, in the United Kingdom, the Muslim Council of Great Britain (the main government-recognized Muslim organization), is led by Islamists. In Spain, leaders of the *Unión de Comunidades Islámicas de España* [Union of Islamic Communities of Spain] (UCIDE)—one of the two federations that compose the government-recognized Islamic Commission of Spain—have close ties with the Syrian Muslim Brotherhood. In France, radicals took control of a new government-sponsored organization, the French Council for

---

[20] Amr Hamzawy, presentation, CSID, Washington, D.C., May 19, 2005.

[21] Author's discussion with CSID president Radwan Masmoudi, Washington, D.C., May 19, 2005.

the Muslim Religion, following elections held in April 2003 in radical-controlled mosques.

Like the argument for engaging Islamists, the argument against engaging them has three parts. First, we do not know whether the Islamists' pro-democracy rhetoric and relatively more moderate discourse represent a strategic or a tactical shift. Have they ceased to be true Islamists, in the sense that they have accepted the separation of religion and the state? Or are they simply lowering the profile of one goal (the establishment of an Islamic state) and emphasizing a more appealing and less controversial agenda? Without a fundamental and demonstrable change in their outlook, what guarantees are there that if Islamists came to power they would not revert to a more radical agenda? Iran provides a cautionary example.

The second argument is that even if Islamists might be more effective in the short term in dissuading potential jihadists from committing acts of terrorism (a questionable proposition to begin with), official recognition and support would enhance their credibility and enable them to proselytize more effectively in the community. Over the long term, the social costs of the spread of the Salafi movement to the masses would be very high.

Third, even if one concedes that in many parts of the Muslim world moderate and liberal groups are organizationally weak and have been as yet unable to develop substantial constituencies, for the West to bypass these groups in favor of Islamist interlocutors would simply perpetuate these weaknesses. One presumption of this study is that the primary weakness of these groups is organizational and that linking them together in robust networks would amplify their message, broaden their appeal, and enable them to compete more effectively with Islamist groups in the political marketplace.

This is not to say that the United States and its partners should not enter into a dialogue with moderate Islamists; such a dialogue could be constructive in clarifying the positions of both sides. However, capacity-building programs and resources are better directed at moderate and liberal Muslim organizations.[22]

Delivering Support to Moderates

Concerns quickly arise whenever the topic of assisting Muslim moderates comes up, such as the question of whether Western backing will discredit them. These questions reflect a somewhat unrealistic notion of political conflict. In conflict, no weapon or strategy is perfect. This is precisely what makes it a conflict—the enemies confront each other, with both sides trying to discover and exploit the limits and failings of the weapons and strategies of the other. Extremists face risks and operate in the face of significant obstacles. The same is true of moderates. Will attempts be made to discredit them as Western tools? Of course, just as the extremists are tarnished in the view of many mainstream Muslims by their use of terrorist tactics and their radical and exclusionary interpretations of Islam.

There are also indications that the problem may be overstated. Several prominent moderates have gone on record as welcoming U.S. support. For example, Saad Eddin Ibrahim, the jailed Egyptian activist who was eventually freed through U.S. intervention, observes that he "appreciated every bit of support I received." Similarly, the prominent writer Naguib Mahfouz rhetorically asked, "What's wrong if the Americans want us to have democracy? Sometimes our interests can coincide."[23]

These questions are easier to resolve when placed in a broader historical context. Recalling the Cold War example, dissidents were indeed jailed, persecuted, and sometimes killed. Staunch leftists and Com-

---

[22] In a *Washington Quarterly* article, scholar Daniel Brumberg argues that uncritical engagement with Islamists in the cause of democracy would strengthen illiberal Islamist forces, particularly in the absence of institutional reform that would prod mainstream Islamists to forge a democratic power-sharing accommodation with regime and with non-Islamist political forces. Daniel Brumberg, "Islam Is Not *the* Solution (or *the* Problem)," *The Washington Quarterly*, Vol. 29, No. 1, Winter 2005–2006.

[23] Cited in Lee Smith, "The Kiss of Death?" *Slate,* November 24, 2004.

munists saw the dissidents as puppets—or, in the language of the day, as the "lackeys" and "stooges" of the imperialists. This is the nature of an ideological conflict. For many Communists, their ideology was not something imposed from above, but an authentically held belief system that contained such notions as justice, equality, and brotherhood. The distance from "scientific socialism" to religion is not so great.

The key question, of course, is not whether, but *how* to channel our assistance and engage prospective partners effectively. Outside support of Muslim moderates is an exceedingly sensitive matter in Islamic countries. Assistance from international sources must be channeled in ways that are appropriate to local circumstances and, to the extent possible, must rely on NGOs that have existing relationships in the recipient countries. The Asia Foundation, which has worked successfully with partners in several Southeast Asian countries, is careful to support indigenous initiatives and is selective about the organizations with which it works. The key success is to engage credible partners while keeping the foreign dimensions of the support effort very much in the background.[24]

This effort could be prioritized in three ways: in terms of partners, programs, and regional focus.

Partners

In the context of today's Muslim world, the potential target groups fall into a number of categories:

Liberal and Secular Muslim Academics. Liberals tend to gravitate toward universities and academic and research centers, from where they can influence opinion. As there are existing networks of liberal and moderate intellectuals throughout the Muslim world, this sector is the primary building bloc for an international moderate Muslim network.

Young Moderate Clerics. One of the reasons for the radicals' success in propagating their ideas is that they use mosques as their vehicles for proselytizing and recruiting. Liberal academics, on the other hand, are not comfortable engaging people at the mosques. They find it dif-

---

[24] RAND discussion in Jakarta, August 2005.

ficult to translate the language of scholarship to which they are accustomed to the language of the average person on the street. Therefore, a liberal or moderate Muslim movement with a mass base will depend on enlisting the active participation of moderate clerics, particularly of young clerics, who will become the religious leadership of the future.

Community Activists. The muscle of this initiative, community activists propagate the ideas developed by liberal and moderate intellectuals. They take real personal risks by confronting often-violent extremists in the battle of ideas, and are the victims of *fatwas* and violent attacks. These groups, therefore, are most in need of the protection and support that an international network can provide. For example, activists in Indonesia's Liberal Muslim Network have taken a high-profile stand against Islamist extremism and have been subjected to a campaign of harassment and intimidation.

Women's Groups. Women and religious minorities have the most to lose from the spread of fundamentalist Islam and rigid interpretations of *shari'a*. In some countries women are beginning to organize to protect their rights from the rising tide of fundamentalism and are becoming an increasingly important constituency of reformist movements in Muslim countries. Groups and organizations have emerged to advance women's rights and opportunities in the areas of legal rights, health, education, and employment.[25] This upsurge in women's civil-society groups in turn provides opportunities for moderate network-building.

Journalists, Writers, and Communicators. Through the use of the Internet and other new media outside of governments' control, radical messages have penetrated deeply into Muslim communities around the world. U.S. funded broadcasting efforts, such as Radio Sawa and Al Hurra television, lack the agility to address local concerns and issues and, in any event, are not working to foster the development of moderate local media outlets. To reverse radical trends in the Muslim media, therefore, it will be critical to support local moderate radio and television programming, as well as Web sites and other nontraditional media.

---

[25] See Satloff, 2004, pp. 83–84.

Programmatic Priorities

The programs directed at the above audiences should have the following foci: democratic education, media, gender equality, and policy advocacy.

Democratic Education. The narrowly sectarian and regressive instruction on religion and politics dispensed at radical and conservative *madrasas*[26] needs to be countered by a curriculum that promotes democratic and pluralistic values. As in many other areas where religion and society intersect, Indonesia is a leader in democratic religious education. The State Islamic University and Muhammadiyah educational systems have developed textbooks to teach civil education in an Islamic context. The courses are mandatory for all students attending these universities.

Some Muslim teachers, although of a moderate disposition, lack the ability to link Islamic teachings explicitly with democratic values. In response, the Asia Foundation has developed a program to assist the efforts of moderate *ulama* to mine Islamic texts and traditions for authoritative teachings that support democratic values. The result is a corpus of writings on *fiqh* (Islamic jurisprudence) that support democracy, pluralism, and gender equality. These texts are on the cutting edge of progressive Muslim thinking and are in great demand internationally.

Institutions like the Nahdlatul Ulama–based Institute for Islamic and Social Studies (LKiS) hold that instead of creating specifically Islamic schools, Muslims should ensure that all institutions are infused with values of social justice and tolerance. The "i" in LKiS (which stands for Islam) is deliberately written in lower case to underscore that LKiS is against the type of Islamism that emphasizes Islam's superiority over other religions. LKiS is currently involved in human-rights training in *pesantren,* the Indonesian Islamic boarding schools.[27]

The outcome of this work is the emergence in Indonesia of a coherent Muslim democracy movement with some unique features: (1) male

---

[26] The Arabic plural of *madrasa* is *madari*, but we anglicize it to *madrasas* in this report.

[27] Ken Miichi, "Islamic Movements in Indonesia," *IIAS Newsletter*, No. 32, November 2003.

ulama who campaign for gender equality; and (2) roots in mass-based organizations, giving the movement the capacity to reach a wide section of the populace at the grass-roots level in a way that urban-based secular groups cannot.

Media. The dissemination of information throughout most of the Muslim world is dominated by anti-democratic radical and conservative elements. In fact, there is no moderate media in some countries. A moderate alternative to the radical media is a critical tool in the war of ideas. Again, Indonesia provides a model, with numerous examples of moderate media:

- The Liberal Muslim Network's weekly radio program, "Religion and Tolerance," reaches approximately 5 million listeners through 40 radio stations nationwide.
- The Institute for Citizens' Advocacy and Education produces a weekly radio talk show that reaches one million listeners through five radio stations in the province of South Sulawesi.
- The national television station, TPI, features a weekly call-in show on gender equality and Islam that reaches 250,000 viewers in the greater Jakarta area.
- A monthly television talk show on Islam and pluralism reaches 400,000 viewers in Yogyakarta.[28]

These moderate media have had an impact in changing the tenor of Islamic discourse in Indonesia. The Islamist media have been forced to address issues that have been raised by the moderate media, such as the status of women's rights.

Gender Equality. The issue of women's rights is a major battleground in the war of ideas currently underway in the Muslim world. As a 2005 Freedom House report stated, the Middle East is the region "where the gap between the rights of men and those of women is the most visible and significant and where resistance to women's equality

---

[28] Asia Foundation, "Islam and Development in Indonesia," Web page, n.d.; United States–Indonesia Society, "Muslim Civil Society," Web page, n.d.

has been most challenging."[29] Some have argued that the subordination of women is central to the whole structure of radical and conservative Islam. Promotion of gender equality is a critical component of any project to empower moderate Muslims. Anat Lapidot-Firilla, academic director of the "Democratization and Women Equity" project at Hebrew University, states that there is an apparent correlation between the status and participation of women and the degree of democracy and political stability in a society. "Today," he says, "not only are women seen as principal agents of democratization and cultural change but also, in the absence of other social movements, women's groups provide the main impetus for expanding citizenship rights, building civil society, and implementing progressive reforms."[30]

The trends in women's empowerment in the Muslim world are mixed, however. In some Southeast Asian countries, women have made important strides in advancing an agenda of gender equality. Ibu Nuriyah, wife of former Indonesian president Abdurrahman Wahid, has published exegetical studies aimed at combating polygamy through the reinterpretation of Quranic concepts and injunctions. She concludes that the Quranic ideal is monogamy and that a woman's right to freely choose a spouse should not be restricted. Some Nahdlatul Ulama–affiliated *pesantren* have established crisis centers for victims of domestic violence. Four members of the fatwa committee of the *Majlis Ulama Indonesia* [Council of Indonesian Ulama] are women, including the noted Quran reciter Maria Ulfa, who has published a treatise on women's issues in *fiqh*. Women in Indonesia also serve as *shari'a* judges and have been accepted as members of the Central Board of the modernist mass organization Muhammadiyah.[31] There are a growing number

---

[29] Sameena Nazir, "Challenging Inequality: Obstacles and Opportunities Towards Women's Rights in the Middle East and North Africa," in *Women's Rights in the Middle East and North Africa*, Washington, D.C.: Freedom House, 2005.

[30] Liora Hendelman-Baavur, Nabila Espanioly, Eleana Gordon, Anat Lapidot-Firilla, Judith Colp Rubin, and Sima Wali, "Women in the Middle East: Progress or Regress? A Panel Discussion" *MERIA Journal*, Vol. 10, No. 2, June 2006.

[31] Oddbjørn Leirvik, "Report from a Delegation Visit to Indonesia by the Oslo Coalition of Freedom of Religion or Belief," July 29–August 11, 2002.

of NGOs that promote gender equity in the Muslim world, such as Rahima and Fahmina in Indonesia and Sisters in Islam in Malaysia.

In other parts of the Muslim world, the growing strength of fundamentalism—especially the codification of *shari'a* in local and national legislation—threatens a retrogression in the position of women in society. In many Muslim countries there is no civil law with regard to personal status (marriage, divorce, child custody, inheritance, etc.) and women are subject to discriminatory treatment under *shari'a*. Regimes that suppress democratic reform also suppress the efforts of women's-rights activists to organize and network. Nabila Espanioly, a clinical psychologist and director of a women's center in Nazareth, says that women can make a change, but only when they understand how to network and to "act against the hierarchy of suffering, which today is one of the major obstacles before women's solidarity and networking."[32]

Policy Advocacy. Islamists use *da'wa* (Islamic proselytizing—literally, "the call") as policy advocacy: In addition to transforming the individual, the goal is to attain social and political objectives, which in the Islamists' view are undistinguishable from religious objectives. Islamists almost always advocate the application of *shari'a*, including, in some cases, its criminal-law component and associated corporal punishments *(hudud)*.

Moderate, liberal, and secular Muslims need to engage in policy advocacy as well. Where Islamists are campaigning for the codification of their particular interpretation of Islam, moderate Muslims need to campaign against legislative discrimination and intolerance. Public-interest advocates and advocacy groups (human-rights activists, corruption watchdogs, think tanks, etc.) have, in fact, multiplied throughout the Muslim world in recent years. These groups can help to shape a political and legal environment that, in turn, can accelerate the development of democratic civil-society institutions.

Regional Focus

This study is focused on network-building opportunities in the Muslim diaspora communities in Europe, Muslims in Southeast Asia, and some

---

[32] Hendelman-Baavur et al., 2006.

of the relatively more open societies in the Middle East. Our focus on
these regions is dictated by the existence of a critical mass of moderate
Muslim institutions and ideas in these regions.

Although many Western initiatives to engage Muslims have a
Middle East focus, in our view the Middle East, and particularly the
Arab world, offers less fertile ground for moderate network and institution building than other regions of the Muslim world. As noted in
other RAND research, while Latin America, Asia, Eastern Europe,
and even parts of sub-Saharan Africa experienced a strong democratic
trend in the 1980s and 1990s, most Arab countries remained mired in
dictatorship and in the politics of violence and exclusion.[33] It is not a
coincidence that the most radical ideologies have emanated from the
Arab world and radiated outward toward other regions of the Muslim
world.

That said, the Arab world is by no means monolithic, and there
are democratizing trends at work in the region that offer the prospect
of transformation. In some countries—Morocco, Jordan, some of the
Gulf states—some democratic elements have been introduced and tolerant interpretations of Islam prevail. Therefore, despite the generally
unpromising prospects, there should be a component of this project
to link the small secular and liberal Muslim groups in the Arab world
with each other and with compatible groups outside the region. Despite
the continuing violence and a strong Islamist trend within both the
Shi'ite and Sunni communities there, Iraq should not be neglected in
this effort.

The thrust of our approach is twofold. The first is to work with
Muslim moderates in countries where conditions are more favorable
to the development of robust moderate Muslim networks and institutions in order to strengthen these societies against the flow of extreme
Salafist interpretations of Islam emanating from the Middle East. The
second is to create channels of communications that will encourage
the dissemination of modern and mainstream interpretations of Islam
back into the Middle East from moderate Muslims elsewhere. Success
in these two areas would hopefully lead to a more balanced equation

---

[33] Rabasa et al., 2003, p. 33.

in which the outflow of radical ideas from the Middle East is counter-balanced by the inflow of more moderate ideas from more enlightened regions of the Muslim world.

As stated above, the Muslim diaspora communities in Europe are an obvious choice as the focus of this effort. Although Muslims in Europe have suffered a variety of ills, including inconsistent approaches to integration by European states, alienation from their national societies, and growing radicalism among second- and third-generation European Muslims, diaspora Muslims are key partners in the effort to build bridges to other parts of the Muslim world for a number of reasons: their familiarity with Western societies, their exposure to liberal democratic values, and their success in maintaining a Muslim identity in a pluralistic society. The noted Malaysian intellectual Chandra Muzaffar captured this when he identified Muslim communities in the West as agents of change within Islam:

> Why in the West? Because in the West, you're challenged intellectually. You have to define your position. You have to try to understand some of your own precepts and principles. And that sort of intellectual challenge is very, very important. It's something that is not happening in the Muslim majority societies where you have this very sort of complacent attitude, where thought has stultified. You find that creativity is no longer there. It's all ossified. But in the West, it's different. They're challenged; they'll have to respond to it.[34]

Southeast Asian Muslims also offer an obvious area of focus. Although the region is often overlooked in discourse about Islam, Southeast Asia is home to one of the largest concentrations of Muslims in the world. Indonesia, the region's largest country, is the world's most populous Muslim-majority country. Moreover, the cultural, ethnic, and religious diversity of the region (in particular the presence of substantial non-Muslim communities) underlies the famously tolerant character of the Southeast Asian practice of Islam. Southeast Asian Muslims are accustomed to coexisting with other cultural and religious

---

[34] Chandra Muzaffar, interview, *Frontline*, October 10, 2001.

traditions. Even more relevant to this project is Southeast Asia's dense structure of moderate Muslim institutions, probably unparalleled in the Muslim world. On the other hand, cultural differences may hinder the ability of Southeast Asian networks to have an impact on Islam in the Arab Middle East.

Obstacles to a Regional Approach

Reversing the flow of radical ideas from the Arab world to the non-Arab regions of the Muslim world will be a formidable challenge because of the lack of Arab civil-society institutions that could act as disseminators of moderate ideas and because of cultural resistance within the Arab world to interpretations of Islam that originated outside the Middle East.

Although the most innovative thinking about Islam is taking place outside the Arab world, Arab institutions hold pride of place in Islamic scholarship. Even within Southeast Asia, the reference points for theologians and educators are al-Azhar and other Middle Eastern universities. For instance, there are more Indonesian students at al-Azhar than at Malaysia's International Islamic University, and few Filipino Muslims are aware that Indonesia is a center of Islamic theological study. Europe lacks institutes for the training of imams, and European Muslim communities are consequently dependent on imams trained in the Middle East and Southeast Asia. Not only do these individuals in many cases lack an understanding of the social conditions in European Muslim communities, but the Islamist viewpoint of some Islamic leaders in Europe actually retards the development of a European Islam consonant with modern values.

Some question whether, in fact, the Islam as practiced in non-Arab regions is transferable to the Arab world. They argue that mass-based Muslim organizations in non-Arab countries, (e.g., in Indonesia or Turkey) do not have counterparts in the Middle East. In fact, Muslim civil-society institutions prominently present in Southeast Asia are the essential moderating elements missing from society in the Middle East. On the other hand, as we will discuss in Chapter Eight, there are emerging elements of civil society in the Middle East that could be linked to networks focused on democratization and the promotion of moderate and liberal Islam.

In disseminating moderate ideas, it is important to introduce Western and Southeast Asian Muslim intellectuals to other regions of the Muslim world and to translate their works into English and Arabic. Indonesians believe that Arab prejudice can be overcome if their ideas are presented in Arabic. At present, there is little systematic translation from Bahasa Indonesia into English and Arabic. The North Carolina–based Libforall Foundation is helping to translate books and articles by progressive Indonesian Muslims into Arabic and English and publishes them on the Internet, as well as in traditional book form.[35] Nevertheless, important works, such as former Muhammadiyah chairman Ahmad Syafii Maarif's recent book *Mencari Autentisitas* [Searching for Authenticity],[36] and many of the publications of the think tanks associated with Indonesia's mainstream Muslim organizations, such as Muhammadiyah's Center for the Study of Religion and Civilization, remain unavailable to those who do not speak Bahasa.

---

[35] Among the works translated and made available by the Libforall Foundation are: *Islamic Law on the Fringe of the Nation State*, by Azyumardi Azra; *The Contextualization of Islamic Law*, by Zainun Kamal; *The Ideal State from the Perspective of Islam and Its Implementation in the Present Age*, by Masyukuri Abdillah; *Islam, the State and Civil Society: The Christian and Muslim Experience*, by Olaf Schumann; *The Secularization of Society and the Indonesian State*, by Yudi Latif; *Democracy and Religion: The Existence of Religion in Indonesian Politics*, by Bahtiar Effendy; *The Role of Telematics in the Democratization of Muslim Nations*, by Marsudi W. Kisworo; *The Impact of Misunderstandings Between Islam and the West*, by Mun'im A. Sirry; *The Democracy Deficit in the Islamic World*, by Sukidi Mulyadi; *Is Religious Jurisprudence Still Relevant? New Perspectives in Political Islamic Thought*, by Luthfi Assyaukanie; *The Jurisprudence of Civil Society Versus the Jurisprudence of Power: A Bid to Reform Political Islam*, by Zuhairi Misrawi; *Reforming Islamic Family Law in Indonesia*, by Siti Musdah Mulia; *Good Governance in Islam: Concepts and Experience*, by Andi Faisal Bakti; *Staking Out the Principles of an Alternative Islamic Jurisprudence*, by Abd Moqsith Ghazali; *Islamic Feminist Movements and Civil Society*, by Nurul Augustina; *Leaving Contemporary Islam, Heading in the Direction of a Different Islam*, by M. Qasim Mathar; *Avoiding "Bibliolatry": The Importance of Revitalizing Our Understanding of Islam*, by Ulil Abshar-Abdalla; *HAM [Indonesian Human Rights Association] and the Problem of Cultural Relativity*, by Budhy Munawar-Rachman; and *The Typology of Contemporary Islamic Movements in Indonesia*, by Komaruddin Hidayat and Ahmad Gaus AF.

[36] Ahmad Syafii Maarif, *Mencari Autenisitas Dalam Kegalauan*, Jakarta: PSAP, 2004.

Another practical difficulty is that in many cases moderate Islam is rooted in local culture, which is very different from the deracinated and globalized Islam of the Salafis. For instance, the Turkish mass-based Gulen movement advocates a Sufi-influenced "Turkish Islam" that may be difficult to propagate outside of the Turkish cultural zone.

The Role of American Muslims

This project focuses on building international networks and does not cover the U.S. Muslim community. Nevertheless, just as U.S. institutions and personalities played an important role in the network-building effort during the Cold War, so do American Muslims have a potentially important role to play in building moderate Muslim networks and institutions. The United States has been more successful in integrating its Muslim population than European nations—the United States is historically a country where successive waves of immigrants have reinvented themselves as Americans. Moreover, American Muslims are well educated—a majority are college graduates—and have annual incomes greater than the average American income.[37] Of course, the American Muslim community is not immune to the global conflict of ideas within Islam. Like other minority Muslim communities, it is subject to radical influences from abroad. For example, a 2005 Freedom House study documented the continued propagation of intolerant Wahhabi ideology in a dozen American mosques and Islamic study centers.[38]

Nevertheless, the vast majority of American Muslims hold values that reflect the democratic and pluralistic political culture of the United States. Therefore, American Muslims, with their cultural knowledge and family and social links to their home countries, could be a critical vector in the war of ideas within the Muslim world. We advocate

---

[37] Project MAPS and Zogby International, *American Muslim Poll 2004*, October 2004.

[38] Center for Religious Freedom, *Saudi Publications on Hate Ideology Fill American Mosques*, Washington, D.C.: Freedom House, 2005.

involving moderate U.S. Muslim groups and organizations, with the safeguards discussed earlier in this report, as an intrinsic component of our proposed network-building initiative.

CHAPTER SIX

The European Pillar of the Network

Europe is home to the world's largest Muslim diaspora community. As a conservative estimate, there are at least 15 million Muslims in Western Europe, with some sources estimating higher numbers still. The largest Muslim concentrations are in France, with between four and six million Muslims, mostly of North African origin; Germany, with over three million, the majority of Turkish ancestry; the United Kingdom, with one and a half million Muslims, predominantly of Southeast Asian origin; Spain, with possibly as many as one million, largely from North Africa; and the Netherlands, with an estimated 920,000, mostly of Turkish and Moroccan origin.[1] There are also notable Muslim concentrations in Italy, Belgium, Austria, and Switzerland. Muslims, of course, have been present in the Balkans since Ottoman times, constituting majorities in Bosnia, Albania, and Kosovo and significant minorities in Bulgaria, Croatia, and Greece.

The intellectual weight of the Muslim diaspora in the West is potentially very great. London is the intellectual, cultural, and media center of the Arab world. In 2004, more books in Arabic were published in Britain and France than in the entire Arab world.[2] Of course, there has been a significant spread of extremist Islamist ideologies among sectors of Europe's Muslim communities, and Europe has emerged as a major theater of jihadist operations. Nevertheless, Europe is also home

---

[1] Statistics Netherlands, *Statline*, electronic database, 2005.

[2] "Islam in Europe: Political & Security Issues for Europe; Implications for the United States," workshop, CNA Corporation's Center for Strategic Studies, January 14, 2005.

to moderate Muslim organizations and to notable moderate Muslim intellectuals and community leaders who are well acquainted with and supportive of liberal Western values and institutions. The increasing weight of Europe's Muslim populations at the point of encounter between the West and the Muslim world makes moderate European Muslims a critical component of our proposed initiative to build moderate Muslim networks.

Contending Visions of Islam in Europe

A range of competing viewpoints has emerged in the struggle to define the nature of Islam and Islamic practice in Europe. It is helpful to categorize these according to the outcomes they favor, or what we might call their vision. Some believe that the natural development for European Muslims—barring the interference of reactionary forces—is to become fully integrated members of European societies and of Western modernity. Like their non-Muslim counterparts, fully integrated Muslims can choose to exercise varying degrees of personal and collective religiosity and personal preferences of diet and conduct that remain confined to the home and to religious locations such as mosques. Adherents of this vision believe that nearly anything a present-day Muslim who has chosen to live in the West might reasonably wish to do in the exercise of his or her faith can be accommodated within the existing social framework.

Other European Muslims believe that, while Muslims should integrate to the extent that they obtain a good education, enter the workplace, and participate in public life, ideally they would maintain a distinct identity within European societies. Their profession of Islam should be known and visible to others, and European society should make suitable adaptation to accommodate it. This group accepts that some Islamic practices may have to be modified to conform to European laws and values. However, adherents of this view believe that Muslims' differences from the majority society should be viewed positively both as cultural enrichment and as a bridge to the larger Muslim world. In their eyes, a moderate and modernized Islam that still remains true to its core principles will ultimately assist in the modernization of the Muslim world.

The third, least integration-minded position holds that Muslims should remain a distinct community, following as much as possible not only their own traditional practices but also their own religious law (*shari'a*), which should be implemented in parallel with Western legal codes. Adherents of this approach generally follow Salafi interpretations of Islam and Islamist political ideologies. Whereas integration-minded Muslims accept, and even welcome, some separate institutions such as Islamic schools and community centers (but not *shari'a* courts), very much like the Protestant and Catholic communities often have their own schools and institutions that function as a part of a pluralistic society, the Salafi sector believes that Muslim institutions should expand until more and more of the Muslims are able to live in an autonomous, discrete world of Islamic practices existing within the secular state. They further believe that through *da'wa*, the higher birth rates of their generally younger population, and continued immigration, the Muslim community will continue to expand and exercise ever greater influence within the society. In other words, while those among the first current of opinion and some adherents of the second favor the Europeanization of Islam, the third current looks forward to the Islamization of Europe.

Each of these three positions, including nonviolent Salafis and Islamists, is considered moderate by the standards of European governments and elites (standards that usually consist of some form of opposition to violence) and worth supporting as a hedge against the undesirable alternative of violent radicalism. From the standpoint of this study, which seeks to identify and support the construction of moderate Muslim networks, the obvious partners in Europe are adherents of the first two approaches. Muslims that favor integration into European societies are also the most likely to share the values and perspectives that we described earlier in this study as characteristic of liberal and moderate Muslims.

Each of these visions is represented by local figures and leaders. Each has allies within European societies and governments, and each has obtained some degree of official backing and support. Nevertheless, we have not encountered any instances of a serious analytic effort on the part of European policymakers or experts to assess the respective costs and benefits of engaging adherents of the different visions, to determine the feasibility of significantly strengthening the first and second visions, or to explore the steps and investments needed to influence the contest of ideas within their Muslim communities in a particular direction. Indeed, a large number of Muslim counterpart organizations recognized by European governments posture themselves as moderate, but are in fact Salafist in orientation or have links to extremist groups.

The case of Nadeem Elyas, former head of the official German *Zentralrat der Muslime in Deutschland*, presents an example of how difficult it can be to assess the true posture of self-identified moderates. In his public statements in the German press, Elyas—sarcastically referred to as the "darling of the dialogue crowd" by the newspaper *Die Welt*—skirts issues such as whether it would be desirable for *shari'a* law to be an option for Muslims in Europe (or even seems to answer them in the negative, saying that it is irrelevant to discuss *shari'a* law, since its application requires an Islamic state, which does not exist in Germany). On his Web site, however, *shari'a* law is described as eternal and binding on all Muslims.[3] Asked about polygamy, he will say only that one does not need to push for its recognition in Europe since it is "not an Islamic duty"; about Islamic penalties such as stoning, that these "could be open to discussion." Elyas neither openly endorses nor directly renounces these practices.

Given the catalytic effect of the Danish cartoon controversy on Muslim anger, it is instructive to look to Denmark and Imam Abu Laban, head of the Islamic Society of Denmark, for another example of a false moderate. Months after the cartoons appeared in the Danish newspaper *Jylland Posten*, Abu Laban led a delegation to various countries in the Arab world. The itinerary included Egypt (for meetings with the Arab League and al-Azhar) and Qatar (for a session with Salafist television preacher Yussuf al-Qaradawi). The intention of this trip was,

---

[3]   Von Anatol, "Mit Gemäßigten Wie Diesen" ["With Moderates Like These"], *Die Gazette*, December 23, 2001.

in the words of Abu Laban himself, to "internationalize the issue" of the cartoons.[4] As has since become known, the delegation added three highly offensive cartoons of unknown provenance to the file it carried to the region and falsely passed them off as part of the Danish series.

Selecting Appropriate Partners

Liberal writers and academics seek to reach an audience, first, through teaching, and they often attract a following of like-minded students. Second, they publish books, editorials, and newspaper columns and are frequent commentators of relevant news events. Third, they found groups and organizations. Fourth, they publish manifestos and platforms or launch signature campaigns on specific issues or on general matters of principle.

A good way to identify moderates is through their identification with the concept of "Euro-Islam." Liberal Muslims champion the development of Euro-Islam as an independent new manifestation of Islam within Western modernity. An example is the Euro Islam Project, a student initiative sponsored by the pro–European Union European Students' Forum AEGEE.[5] The group sponsors workshops, student exchanges, lecture events, and publications aimed at defining and promoting a specifically European, modern Islam that retains an Islamic character yet is open to the surrounding society.

The group's vision is shared by journalists, intellectuals, academics, and activists, as well as a growing number of politicians. Examples of the latter include Nasser Khader, MP with the Danish Social Liberal Party, and Rachid Kachi, MP with the French Union for a Popular Movement Party. Born in Damascus to a Palestinian father and Syrian mother, Khader settled in Denmark with his working-class parents as a small child; he has published a book recounting the story of his per-

---

[4] Ayman Qenawi, "Danish Muslims 'Internationalize' Anti-Prophet Cartoons," *IslamOnline.net*, November 18, 2005.

[5] For more information see the group's Web page "EuroIslam."

sonal integration into European society.[6] He is the founder of Democratic Muslims and its civil-society counterpart, the Danish Support Network for Democratic Muslims. Reportedly, Khader has been the target of death threats, including a call to kill him issued by Imam Ahmad Akkari, one of the group of Danish imams behind the cartoon controversy.[7] Rachid Kaci, an immigrant to France from the Kabylie region of Algeria and the president of the organization *La Droite Libre*, which he runs together with Alexandre Del Valle, is an outspoken critic of Islamism, editorialist, and author.

Samia Labidi, originally from Tunis, heads a group called A.I.M.E., which describes itself as "cultural" and "apolitical." Labidi's goal, according to one biographical profile, is to give a stronger voice to the "silent majority" of moderate Muslims in Europe.[8] Among other activities, the group publishes a visually appealing, entertaining, and sophisticated quarterly magazine, *Electrochoc*. The Spring 2006 issue featured, among other things, a lengthy profile of Muriel Degauque, the Belgian convert to Islam who became a suicide bomber in Iraq; an article about Sikhs and their feelings about the French ban on visible signs of religious affiliation in public schools; and a fabricated interview in which the Prophet Muhammad answers questions on a range of current issues.[9] The format and content of the publication are designed to appeal to a young, non-academic yet urban and relatively educated readership.

---

[6]   Naser Khader, *Khader.dk: Sammenførte Erindringer*, [Copenhagen]: Aschehoug, 2000.

[7]   The threat was filmed by journalist Sifaoui with a hidden camera and broadcast on French television (France 2, *Envoye Special*, television broadcast, March 23, 2006). Khader has required police guard since founding the Democratic Muslims. He describes the stress on himself and his family caused by the threatening phone calls, messages, and restrictions on his freedom of movement in a television interview. Ahmad Akkari, interview on *TV-Avisen*, Denmark Radio, April 2, 2006. Transcribed and translated at Weblog "Agora."

[8]   See A.I.M.E. Web site.

[9]   In the "interview," moderate and modernist views are attributed to the Prophet. Asked about the Muslim practice of child marriage, for example, he replies that during his own times, norms were different and life expectancy was much lower, so that the age of the majority was considerably younger than today. Asked for his views on bin Laden, he replies, "In the 14th century, he would have made a fine Muslim. Today, he is nothing more than an ordinary criminal who has no understanding of the age he lives in." *Electrochoc*, Spring 2006.

There are also important moderate Muslims in the European academic community. For example, Afshin Ellian, who came to the Netherlands as a refugee from Iran, completed his studies in the Netherlands and is now a professor of law at the University of Leiden and a columnist for the Amsterdam-base liberal daily newspaper *Handelsblad*. His tone is generally temperate, but this has not spared him from receiving so many death threats that he must live under police guard.[10]

In Denmark, Professor Mehdi Mozaffari teaches at the University of Aarhus. An Iranian refugee, he was formerly the head of the International Relations Department at Tehran University. He is the initiator of the manifesto "Together Facing a New Totalitarianism" (which, along with the list of first signatories, is reproduced in Appendix B) and is a strong adherent of the school of thought emerging in Europe that sees Islamism as a variant of totalitarianism.

One of the better known European Muslim moderate intellectuals is the German-based professor and writer Bassam Tibi, a frequent presence on the European lecture circuit. As the founder of the Arab Organization for Human Rights and a member of several organizations that promote Muslim-Jewish and Muslim-Christian-Jewish dialogue, he is also strongly supportive of the integration of Muslim minorities into mainstream European society and opposed to parallel legal, cultural, and social systems. With his outspoken belief that immigrants should accept the values of the dominant Western culture (the *Leitkultur*) instead of attempting to subvert or change it and his opposition to a *Parallelgesellschaft* [Parallel Security], he has incurred the animosity of fundamentalists. Tibi differs—persistently and insistently—with the Islamist premise that Islam is necessarily entwined with the public space and with politics; he opposes any inroads of Islamic law in Europe, arguing that "the relationship between *shari'a* and human rights is like that between fire and water."[11]

---

[10] A collection of his newspaper columns can be found at his blog: Afshin Ellian, "About Afshin Ellian."

[11] "Der Multikulturalismus hat dem Scharia: Islam in Europa die Tür Geöffnet," *NZZ am Sontag*, October 2002.

Al-Hadi al-Sabah is the imam of the Passau Mosque in Germany. In his media appearances he regularly condemns terrorism and anti-Christian agitation, questions the qualifications of those who style themselves imams, and disavows the use of violence to solve social and political problems.[12]

Soheib Bencheikh, the Saudi-born, al-Azhar–educated Grand Mufti of Marseille, is considered a leading anti-fundamentalist. His book *Marianne et le Prophete, L'Islam dans la France Laique*[13] highlights the opportunities open to Muslims and to Islamic life within the secular society of France. He can generally be relied upon to provide responses that are acceptable to pious mainstream Muslims without further escalating difficult situations. For example, in the French *hijab* controversy, his view was that Muslim women could be excused from wearing the *hijab* if the surrounding society made it difficult. During the Danish cartoon controversy, he remarked that the cartoons had crossed the line between freedom of expression and respect for religion, but that this was a reflection of the West having lost its spirituality and that violence was not a correct response.

Moderate European Muslim Organizations

Although most European organizations purporting to represent Muslims are Salafi in orientation or are associated with or tolerant of extremist groups, there are some that are unquestionably moderate. Among these is FEERI, which is led by Spanish converts with a moderate orientation. Together with the UCIDE, an organization whose leadership has links to the Syrian Muslim Brotherhood, FEERI is part of the officially recognized Islamic Commission of Spain, which represents Spain's Muslim community to the Spanish government. Both federations are weak financially and largely dependent on funding from the

---

[12] See, for example, his statements in a roundtable on the German government-sponsored Web site *Qantara*.

[13] Soheib Bencheikh, *Marianne et le Prophete, L'Islam dans la France Laique*, Paris: Bernard Grasset Publishers, 1998.

Spanish government; they are seeking, with uncertain success, to reach out to Spain's large Moroccan immigrant population.

FEERI's leader, Mansur Escudero,[14] issued the well-known fatwa declaring bin Laden and al-Qaeda apostates for their terrorist actions, which he stated are contrary to the teachings of Islam. Escudero's argument was that terrorists, by their actions, rejected the word of the Quran and took themselves out of the Muslim community. According to Escudero, the fatwa received discreet support in the Arab world, particularly in North Africa. It was denounced by radicals, and its authority was questioned by others, such as Tariq Ramadan. In fact, whether authoritative or not, the value of the Spanish fatwa may have been in forcing a debate on the obligation of Muslims to expel from the community those who practice terrorism. Beyond opposition to terrorism, Escudero believes that the essence of Islam is democracy and wants to recover the spiritual significance of al-Andalus (Medieval Muslim Spain), which he believes was predicated on freedom of conscience.[15]

FEERI seeks to be involved in international Muslim affairs, but lacks the infrastructure and dedicated personnel to fully exploit its international relations. The organization runs the most popular Muslim Web site in the Spanish-speaking world, www.webislam.com, and publishes *Amanecer* (New Dawn), an English-language journal, to propagate FEERI's moderate interpretation of Islam.

The *Fédération Nationale des Musulmans de France* [National Federation of Muslims of France] (FNMF), headed by the Moroccan Mohamed Bechari, is analogous to Spain's FEERI. The federation is part of the officially recognized *Conseil Française du Culte Musulman* [French Council of the Muslim Religion] (CFCM). In April 2003, the FNMF won 16 seats in the CFCM, out of a total of 41.[16] Bechari is

---

[14] Since this report was written, there was a change of leadership in FEERI. Some of Mansur Escudero's associates have established a new organization, *la Federación Musulmana de España* [the Muslim federation of Spain] (FEME). Escudero remains the co-chairman of FEERI.

[15] Author's discussion with Mansur Escudero, Spain, August 2005.

[16] The radical *Union des Organisations Islamiques de France* won 14 seats, and the more moderate Paris Mosque won six. Two seats went to the *Comité de Coordination des Musulmans*

also Secretary-General of the Paris-based European Islamic Conference. He believes that "the global diversity of Islam" can come together in Europe and provide a new democratic and pluralistic model for the Muslim-majority countries outside the continent.[17] Although financially dependent on Moroccan and Libyan support, the European Islamic Conference, which includes a number of European moderate Muslim organizations, might be an adequate vehicle for the development of the European pillar of an international moderate Muslim network.

In Italy there are a number of moderate Muslim institutions and personalities. The Confederation of Moroccan Associations in Italy is headed by Souad Sbai, a Italian-Moroccan feminist who has been active in the fight against spouse abuse in Italy's Moroccan community. The al-Azhar–educated Sufi sheikh Abdul Hadi Palazzi, another leading moderate, directs the Cultural Institute of the Italian Islamic Community, which promotes the development of Islamic education in Italy, combats fundamentalism and fanaticism, and is involved in interreligious dialogue, especially with Jews and Christians.[18] Regarding the question of the compatibility of Islamic and secular law, Palazzi argues that *shari'a* forbids a Muslim from performing acts—even acts declared permissible in the Quran—that violate the law of the state in which he

---

Turcs de France and the other three to independent groups. Glen Feder, "The Muslim Brotherhood in France," *In the National Interest*, Web site, September 21, 2005.

[17] Mohamed Bechari, "¿Qué lugar ocupará el Islam en la nueva Europa?" *Memoria*, No. 202, December 2005.

[18] Other, less moderate Muslim communities and institutions in Italy are associated with or receive funding from the Saudis. These include the Islamic Cultural Center *(Centro Islamico Culturale d'Italia)*, the institution behind the construction of Rome's massive mosque of Monte Antenne. Financing for the center is being channeled through the Saudi-based World Muslim League *(Rabita al-Alam al-Islami)*. The Islamic Cultural Center and a Syrian-led Italian branch of the Muslim Brotherhood, the Union of Islamic Communities and Organizations of Italy, have joined in an umbrella organization, the Islamic Council of Italy *(Consiglio Islamico d'Italia)*, in order to become the official interlocutor between Italy's Muslims and the Italian state. Another organization competing to represent Islam in Italy, the Islamic Religious Community *(Comunita Religiosa Islamica-COREIS)*, is said to have received substantial Saudi aid. Stefano Allievi, "Islam in Italy," in Shireen Hunter, ed., *Islam, Europe's Second Religion*, Westport and London: Praeger, 2002.

or she lives. Consequently, Muslims must abstain from actions allowed in the Quran when those actions are illegal in a society in which a Muslim lives. In 1996, Palazzi and Israeli scholar Dr. Asher Eder co-founded the Islam-Israel Fellowship to promote cooperation between Israel and Muslim nations, and between Jews and Muslims.[19]

The Muslim Council of Britain (MCB) claims to be the voice of moderate Muslims in the United Kingdom, but its credentials as a moderate organization are suspect.[20] Of the various Muslim organizations in the United Kingdom, the one with the most liberal coloration is Progressive British Muslims. Another moderate organization, the British Muslim Forum, is an umbrella group launched in March 2005 with more than 250 affiliated mosques and other organizations.[21]

---

[19] See interview with Sheikh Abdul Hadi Palazzi in Jamie Glazov, "The Anti-Terror, Pro-Israel Sheikh," *FrontPageMagazine.com*, September 12, 2005.

[20] For instance, a BBC Panorama program aired August 21, 2005, examined an MCB affiliate, The Islamic Foundation, that has strong connections with the extremist Pakistani organization *Jamaat-i-Islami*. Other questionable MBC affiliates, according to MCB Watch, are *Jamiat Ahl-e-Hadith*, which alleges that Jews are trying to take over the world, and the Muslim Association of Britain, which states that suicide attacks against civilians in Israel are acceptable. The MBC also has a history of defending radical Islamists who come under political attack; for instance, the MCB defended the Hizb ut-Tahrir when the Blair government announced its intention to ban that organization. See Muslim Council of Britain, "It Doesn't Add Up," Web log entry, October 29, 2005.

[21] The following aims and objectives of the Forum are outlined on its Web site:
- To communicate the balanced opinions and impartial ways of Islam and promote its peace-loving morals and etiquettes
- To promote values that are common to all humanity through teachings of fearing god and serving humanity as per the education of the Sufiya (spiritual leaders)
- To instill such values in the next generation of Muslims that will lead to improved cohesion in a multi-religious, multi-cultural and multi-racial and intellectually open thinking society
- To support, strengthen and supervise the existing efforts & projects of Muslim females that are acceptable to Islamic regulation
- To strengthen the existing multi-faith links that promotes understanding and tolerance amongst faith communities
- To establish a network of official, political, social and educational organisations of Muslims addressing their problems and concerns and taking appropriate steps to resolve them
- The Forum will work to protect the rights of the affiliate organisations, institutes and mosques and will try to stabilise and improve their educational and financial welfare

The Sufi Council of Britain is currently being formed to challenge the MCB. As of this writing (July 2005) the Sufi Council was about to be launched with a publication and Web site. Also of note is the fact that moderate Muslim leader Fiyaz Mughal is serving as the vice president of Britain's Liberal Democrat Party.

In the Balkans, moderate currents of Islam—particularly Sufism—prevail, although Saudi foundations and missionaries have been active in Bosnia and other parts of the region, and there has been some Wahhabi infiltration of mosques and Islamic institutions.[22] There are a number of important moderate Muslim institutions in the Balkans:

- The Islamic Community of Bosnia-Hercegovina, headed by Reis-ul-Ulema Mustafa ef. Ceric and headquartered in Sarajevo, has responsibility for Muslims in Croatia, Slovenia, and the Sanjak (which is now split between Serbia and Montenegro).
- The Faculty of Islamic Studies and Gazi Husrevbeg Medresa located in Sarajevo is the main Islamic educational institution in Southeastern Europe; it educates most Slavic and Albanian clerics. Bosnia also has the largest Islamic publishing milieu in Europe, especially for European Sufis content.
- The Islamic Community of Kosovo, headed by Reis-ul-Ulema Naim Ternava and headquartered in Prishtina, controls the small but excellent Faculty of Islamic Studies at the University of Prishtina and the Alauddin Medresa. The community administers some 500 mosques.
- The Community of Aliite Islamic Dervishes [of former Yugoslavia], headquartered in Prizren, Kosovo, includes all non-Bektashi Sufis.

- To establish a link with all areas of the media, forwarding to them the concerns and reservations of the Muslims, and to offer through general consensus the endorsed opinions of the Muslims on issues that are of concern to them.
- To take appropriate actions in attempt to reduce or eliminate terrorism, extremism and religious & racial discrimination.

[22] We extend our appreciation to Stephen Schwartz for the information on moderate Muslim communities in the Balkans.

- The Alevian Islamic Community of Albania, headquartered in Tirana, Albania, and headed by Sheh Ali Pazar includes all non-Bektashi Sufis and has created a network of 400 Sufi lodges (or *teqes*).
- The World Bektashi Community, headed by World Dede [Chief Sheikh] Reshat Bardha and headquartered in Tirana, Albania. represents some two million Bektashi adherents of various levels of affiliation, mainly in southern Albania and western Macedonia. Bektashi is a highly heterodox form of Sufism with strong roots in Albanian culture. The Harabati Bektashi *Teqe* in Tetova, Macedonia, is a also major Sufi institution in the Balkans, but it is now under siege by Wahhabis.

CHAPTER SEVEN

The Southeast Asian Pillar of the Network

Network-building efforts in Southeast Asia should incorporate NGO work with the moderate traditionalist Indonesian organization Nahdlatul Ulama, with its 15,000 affiliated *pesantren*, and with the modernist organization Muhammadiyah and its network of higher education and social welfare institutions. Both Islamist and liberal sectors coexist in Muhammadiyah: Islamist elements can be found in the organization's Religious Council, which is charged with *da'wa*, while liberals have a home in the Center for the Study of Religion and Democracy, established to promote a liberal agenda within and outside the organization.

The most unabashedly liberal Muslim organization in Indonesia (and perhaps in all of Southeast Asia) is the Liberal Muslim Network, established in 2001 by young liberal Muslim intellectuals to counter the growing influence and activism of militant and radical Islam in Indonesia. The network's coordinator, Ulil Abshar Abdalla, was the target of a fatwa issued by radical clerics in 2004 for "apostasy." In August 2005, the Indonesian Ulema Council, controlled by radical and conservative elements, issued a fatwa denouncing pluralism, liberalism, and secularism as contrary to Islam.[1] A violent Islamist group, the Islam Defenders Front, used this fatwa as justification to threaten violence against the Liberal Muslim Network.

---

[1] The fatwa was sharply criticized by prominent Indonesian moderate Muslims ranging from former president Abdurrahman Wahid and the leadership of Nahdlatul Ulama to former Muhammadiyah chairman Ahmad Syafii Maarif and Dr. Azyumardi Azra, the rector of the Syarif Hidayatullah State Islamic University.

Within the Muslim areas of the Philippines there has been a remarkable surge of civil-society organizations formed specifically to address the problems of poverty and corruption. The Ulama League of the Philippines is also active in promoting peace and development. The Magbassa Kita Foundation, founded by Santanina Rasul, the only Muslim woman elected to the Philippine Senate, developed a literacy training program that is being implemented nationwide.

According to Jakarta-based NGO staff, moderate Muslim organizations such as Muhammadiyah and Nahdlatul Ulama are transcending sectarian differences to promote democratic values.[2] There is, she says, a gradual consolidation of Muslim NGOs into a cohesive movement. While driven by urban intellectuals, this movement has its roots in the national networks of Muhammadiyah and Nahdlatul Ulama. The key component of these networks is the educational institution.

Moderate Religious Educational Institutions

Islamic Schools (*Pesantren* and *Madrasas*)

There are two kinds of Islamic schools in Southeast Asia: Islamic day schools, known as *madrasas,* and boarding schools, known as *pesantren* (in Indonesia) or *pondok*.[3] The majority of the Indonesian *pesantren* are affiliated with the traditionalist Nahdlatul Ulama organization. In fact, to a large extent Nahdlatul Ulama can be said to be the sum of its *pesantren*. A smaller number of *pesantren* are affiliated with the modernist Muhammadiyah and Persis organizations; only a very small minority of *pesantren* teaches extremist interpretations of Islam.[4] In Indonesia, and to a lesser extent in other Southeast Asian countries, most *pesantren* and *madrasas* include secular subjects in their curri-

---

2   Author's interview in Jakarta, August 2005.

3   For a more extended discussion, see Angel Rabasa, "Islamic Education in Southeast Asia," in Hillel Fradkin, Husain Haqqani, and Eric Brown, eds., *Current Trends in Islamist Ideology*, Vol. 2, Washington, D.C.: Hudson Institute, 2005.

4   Lily Munir, "In Search of a New Islamic Identity in Indonesia," presentation, The United States–Indonesia Society (USINDO) Conference, Washington, D.C., November 11, 2003.

cula; however, their main purpose is to teach Islam. As textbooks are written in Arabic, learning the Arabic language and how to translate those textbooks into the local dialect constitutes a major part of the curriculum.

Pesantren are run and often owned by an individual religious teacher. The students are bound in a personal relationship with their teacher, or *kiai*, who may promote a particular ideology or interpretation of Islam. Many contemporary *pesantren* are now engaging in both traditional Islamic education and modern national education. Nevertheless, even with the addition of secular education, the main purpose of *pesantren*, as noted above, is to spread Islam. The value system taught at *pesantren* defines a modernity quite different from that practiced in the West. The values of Islamic brotherhood and selflessness are seen as safeguards against heartless capitalism. These values are by no means inconsistent with democracy. Over the past decade, over 1,000 *pesantren* have participated in programs to promote values of pluralism, tolerance, and civil society. In one such program, the *pesantren* students are taught to run issue-based campaigns, conduct elections for student leadership, and represent their constituency to both with *pesantren* leaders and the local community.

In Malaysia, by contrast, the Islamist *Parti Islam SeMalaysia* [Islamic Party of Malaysia] (PAS) exercises a strong influence over the system of private Islamic schools. Although the level of militancy in the Malaysian Islamic education system has never approached that of Pakistan, it nevertheless sustains a fundamentalist, politico-religious movement. In the *pondoks* of Southern Thailand, the national curriculum is taught alongside Islamic subjects. While in the past, the Thai *pondoks* helped to preserve the local Malay dialect in Southern Thailand, now instruction is conducted in Thai and in the Arabic needed for the study of the Quran. Nevertheless, *pondoks* in Southern Thailand reportedly serve as recruitment centers for a violent separatist campaign. In the Philippines, the Islamic schools operating within the formal education system—that is, those accredited by the state—are generally moderate, but there are a few unaccredited radical *madrasas*, some funded by the Saudis.[5]

Islamic Universities

Indonesia has the most extensive and sophisticated system of Islamic university education in Southeast Asia—and perhaps in the world. The Syarif Hidayatullah Islamic University, formerly *Institut Agama Islam Negeri* [State Institute for Islamic Studies] (IAIN) system comprises 47 colleges and universities with over 100,000 students. The university has nine faculties, including a Faculty of Theology (*Fakultas Ushuluddin*), which includes a Department of Comparative Religion, a Faculty of *Shari'a* (*Fakultas Syari'ah*), and a Centre for Women's Studies. The IAIN system draws many of its students from the *pesantren* since, until recently, a *pesantren* education did not provide access to other universities.[6] The IAIN publishes the academic journals *Studia Islamika* and *Kultur,* which print articles by Indonesian and Western Islamic scholars. IAIN has long been at the forefront of interfaith dialogue. Perspectives of comparative religion are included in Islamic studies at IAIN, together with interfaith, human rights, and gender issues. The university's overarching aim is producing tolerant graduates with a modern, "rational Islam" outlook.[7]

Another major Islamic university system, with 35 universities and some 160 tertiary institutions, is associated with Muhammadiyah. The Muhammadiyah modeled their educational institutions on the Dutch school system. The Muhammadiyah system teaches the national curriculum, and includes religious subjects that reflect the organization's modernist orientation.

Both the IAIN and Muhammadiyah universities subscribe to democratic and pluralistic values. After the downfall of President

---

[5]   Author's discussion with Amina Rasul-Bernardo, Washington, D.C., April 2005.

[6]   Johan Meuleman, "The Institut Agama Islam Negeri at the Crossroads," in Johan Meuleman, ed., *Islam in the Era of Globalization*, Jakarta: Indonesian-Netherlands Cooperation in Islamic Studies, 2001, pp. 283–288. There are over 100,000 students enrolled in the IAIN system.

[7]   Leirvik, 2006.

Suharto's government in 1998, IAIN developed a course on civic education, replacing the previously mandatory state ideology courses with a new curriculum designed to teach democracy in an Islamic context. This course has been made mandatory for all students in the IAIN system and has proven so successful that the Muhammadiyah network also developed its own mandatory democratic civic education course.[8]

Gadja Madha University in Yogyakarta, Indonesia's oldest university, established a Center for Religious Cross-Cultural Studies at the instigation of former Foreign Minister Alwi Shihab. The center offers comparative religious studies rather than religious studies focusing solely on a single religion, as is the case in other universities.

In Malaysia, the government-supported International Islamic University teaches a universalistic interpretation of Islam that is closer to that of religious institutions in the Arab world. There are some Islamic colleges in the Philippines, but no Islamic university. The Mindanao State University, a secular institution with nine campuses, has a majority Muslim student body. Thailand plans to establish its first Islamic university in 2005, which will be a branch of Egypt's al-Azhar University. The Thai government will provide most of the funding for the project, but the university will seek financial assistance from outside sources, including Muslim countries.[9]

In conclusion, Southeast Asia has an extraordinarily large and well-developed structure of Islamic educational institutions that can be a resource of critical importance in the ongoing war of ideas within the Muslim world, as well as in the effort to build moderate Muslim networks proposed in this study. These institutions will help to keep the Muslim communities in Southeast Asia rooted in their moderate and tolerant values despite the onslaught of extremist ideology from the Middle East; they could also serve as building blocks for an international network of moderate Islamic educational institutions.

---

[8]   The Asia Foundation, "Education Reform and Islam in Indonesia," pamphlet, n.d.

[9]   "Al Azhar to Offer Courses in Thailand," *The Nation* (Bangkok), September 23, 2004.

Media

Moderate and liberal Muslims in Southeast Asia have become much more adept at using the media to respond quickly and effectively to radicals. The Liberal Muslim Network's radio program "Religion and Tolerance" is one of the most popular talk shows in Indonesia. Transcripts from the show have been published in the Jawa Post and syndicated in over 70 newspapers.

Democracy-Building Institutions

Muslim organizations in Indonesia have established institutes to educate their members about democratic processes, such as the *Lembaga Kajian dan Pengembangan Sumberdaya Manusia* [Human Resource Development and Study Institute] and Lakpesdam, a Nahdlatul Ulama institute involved in voter education in East Java with the support of the Asia Foundation and the Ford Foundation. PM3, a *pesantren*-based NGO, conducts discussions in *pesantren* on the Islamic principles that limit the power of the state to regulate religion.[10]

In the Philippines, the most active and effective of these institutions is the Philippine Council for Islam and Democracy (PCID), headed by Amina Rasul-Bernardo, the daughter of former Senator Santanina Rasul, the first Muslim woman elected to the Philippine Senate. The Rasuls derive their influence from their status as descendants of the hereditary prime ministers of the Sultanate of Sulu and from their success in reaching out to Philippine and international civil-society groups and NGOs. Another promising institution, the Consortium of Bangasomoro Civil Society, with headquarters in Cotabato City, is strongest on Mindanao and has succeeded in reaching to a broad spec-

---

[10] United States–Indonesia Society, "Muslim Society and Democracy," report on presentation, Washington, D.C., April 26, 2005. Also, Lilis N. Husna, interview in Ford Foundation, *Celebrating Indonesia: Fifty Years with the Ford Foundation, 1953–2003*, [Jakarta], 2003, p. 213.

trum of Moro communities.[11] The Center for Moderate Muslims, led by Professor Taha Basman, is well established in Manila as well as in Davao City, Zamboanga, and Marawi on Mindanao. The center has a project to develop a directory of mosques and madrasas throughout the country.[12]

Regional Network-Building Efforts

Southeast Asia is the primary regional theater in ongoing efforts to link local and national moderate Muslim networks and organizations to a regional network. Spearheading this effort is the International Center for Islam and Pluralism (ICIP), established in Jakarta with support from the Asia Foundation. ICIP's missions are to build a network of Muslim NGOs and progressive Muslim activists and intellectuals in Southeast Asia (and eventually throughout the world) and to serve as a vehicle for disseminating the ideas of international progressive and moderate Muslim thinkers.[13] ICIP has held regional workshops on Islam and democracy, the first one in Manila together with the PCID in September 2005 and the second one in Jakarta in December 2005. Former Thai Foreign Minister Surin Pitsuwan has suggested using ICIP to link the *pondok* community in Southern Thailand with progressive *pesantren* in Indonesia.[14]

Through these discussions and dialogues, moderate Southeast Asian Muslims have begun to lay out a regional agenda. At the Manila meeting, the participants recommended that an intra-Islamic confer-

---

[11] Author's discussion with Steven Rood, Asia Foundation Philippines Country representative, Manila, August 2005.

[12] Author's discussion with Taha Basman, Manila, August 2005

[13] More information on ICIP can be found at the organization's Web site. ICIP's international board includes prominent Southeast Asian moderate Muslim personalities, including Azyumardi Azra (president of the Indonesian State Islamic University), the late Nurcholish Madjid, Surin Pitsuwan (former Thai Foreign Minister), Zainah Anwar (director of Sisters in Islam), Chandra Muzaffar of Malaysia, and others.

[14] Author's discussion with Asia Foundation Indonesia Country Representative Douglas Ramage, Jakarta, August 2005.

ence or dialogue should be held in the region to discuss the compatibility of Islam and democracy, with particular consideration of democratic values that can be found in the Quran. They underscored the importance of discussing and disseminating Islamic teachings on governance and the principles of democracy; they also recommended that benchmarks on Islam and democracy be established to determine the extent of democratization among Muslim communities. Meeting attendees highlighted the need for collaboration among Muslim communities in the region, and particularly the need for institutions, including centers and organizations, that support regional cooperation. The participants stressed that efforts at cooperation must be cognizant of the cultural peculiarities of Southeast Asia and not simply borrow from the experience of other regions of the Muslim world, such as the Middle East.[15]

---

[15] Philippine Center for Islam and Democracy, "Southeast Asian Muslim Leaders and Scholars Convene on Islam & Democratization," *PCID Policy Report*, Vol. 1, No. 3, December 2005.

CHAPTER EIGHT

The Middle East Component

The principal obstacle to the building of moderate Muslim networks in the Middle East is the lack of extant, widespread liberal movements to network; only small groups and scattered individuals exist there today. According to Muslim liberals in the Middle East, winning the battle for Islam requires the creation of liberal groups "to retrieve Islam from hijackers."[1] There was a certain amount of political pluralism under the Egyptian and Iraqi monarchies, but that was crushed by the military regimes that followed their overthrow in the 1950s. In Egypt, there is the form, but not the substance, of parliamentary government (and not even that in Iraq under Saddam Hussein). In the absence of liberal movements or civil society, Islamists and mosques are the only channel for political dissent. In discussions held with Egyptian liberal intellectuals, they stated that it was important for the United States to help amplify liberal voices and that so doing may raise their visibility at home and internationally. One Egyptian liberal suggested that the United States should develop an intellectual equivalent of the Davos World Economic Forum and build a "liberal international" Web site to provide moral support, links to other Web sites, and forums to facilitate interaction between liberals.[2]

There was consensus among our Egyptian interlocutors that Egyptian Islam is essentially moderate; several contrasted it with the

---

[1] Author's discussion with Dr. Ahmed Bishara, Secretary-General, Kuwait National Democratic Movement, Kuwait, June 2003.

[2] RAND discussions in Cairo, Egypt, June 2003.

Saudi form of Islam. One noted that one of the reasons for the defeat of *al-Gama'a al-Islamiyya,* an extremist offshoot of the Egyptian Muslim Brotherhood, was that it began to interfere with people's traditional customs. However, lacking alternative moderate political outlets, public dissatisfaction with the status quo is channeled through the Muslim Brotherhood and other Islamist factions.

Jordanian society could provide a suitable platform on which to build moderate networks in the Arab world. Dr. Mustafa Hamarneh, Director of the Center for Strategic Studies in Amman, told a RAND researcher in 2003 that "the society is more mature than the government" and that Jordan is at a crossroads where one of its choices is to reform and democratize more rapidly. As a sign of this maturity, Dr. Hamarneh stated that Muslims were increasingly voting for candidates based on issues other than religious affiliation. In this regard, the results of a survey on attitudes affecting voting shared with RAND by Dr. Fares Braizat, Political Director of the Center for Strategic Studies at the University of Jordan, show that personal competence, clan affiliation, and political experience came before religion.[3]

Moderate Islam is the norm in many of the smaller Gulf states such as Kuwait, Bahrain, and Dubai and Abu Dhabi in the United Arab Emirates (UAE), but there are no organized moderate networks. The better-organized Salafi and Wahhabi groups have been making inroads in these states, particularly in the education and financial sectors. For instance, the Muslim Brotherhood controls the Kuwait University administration and the Kuwait Financial House.[4] Nevertheless, despite organizational drawbacks, Kuwaiti liberals are struggling to promote democracy, pluralism, and religious moderation. Among the most notable Kuwaiti liberals are Dr. Ahmed Bishara, Secretary-General of the Kuwait National Democratic Movement; Dr. Shamlan Al-Essa, Director, Center for Strategic and Future Studies, Kuwait

---

[3] RAND discussions with Drs. Hamarneh and Braizat, Amman, June 2003.

[4] RAND interview with Dr. Shamlan Al-Essa, Director, Center for Strategic and Future Studies, Kuwait University, June 2003.

University; and Mohammed Al-Jassem, editor-in-chief of Kuwait's largest-circulation newspaper, *Al-Watan*.[5]

With regard to the development of civil society, the most promising countries, aside from Kuwait, are Bahrain and the UAE. Bahrain has an active civil society. In 2002, the country held its first parliamentary elections in 30 years—also the first elections in which women were allowed to vote and stand for office (although none was elected). However, Islamist parties—the Salafist Asalah, the Shi'ite Islamic Bloc, and the Muslim Brotherhood—dominate the elected lower chamber of parliament. The most important liberal party is the Economists Bloc, which advocates human rights, democratization, and free market economics.[6] In the civil-society sector, the Women's Union of Bahrain, which comprises about a dozen women's associations, was given legal recognition in 2006.[7]

Some of the emirates in the UAE, particularly Dubai and Abu Dhabi, are socially but not politically liberal. According to an Emirati interlocutor, there is a critical mass of moderate and liberal thinkers in the UAE, mostly in academia, but with the exception of the Reform Society of Dubai and the UAE Human Rights Association, they do not have organizational expression.[8] Among prominent moderate Emirati intellectuals are Mohamed Al Roken, Assistant Dean of the Faculty of Sharia Law at the UAE University at Al Ain; Abdul Ghaffar Hussain, Chairman of the UAE Human Rights Association; Muhammad al-Mansouri and Abdulla Al Shamsi, members of the board of directors of the UAE Human Rights Association; and businessman and human rights campaigner Khalifa Bakhit al-Falasi.

---

[5]   RAND discussions in Kuwait, June 2003.

[6]   *Wikipedia*, s.v. "Economists Bloc."

[7]   "Bahrain Women's Union Gets Ministry's Approval," *Khaleej Times,* July, 27, 2006.

[8]   Mohamed Al Roken defines moderates, in the Emirati context, as those who adhere to liberal interpretations of Islam, believe in women's rights, and support dialogue with the West. RAND discussion with Mohamed Al Roken, Dubai, January 2006.

Democracy-Building Projects

A number of Western institutions have been conducting democracy-building projects in the Middle East. The Ibn Rushd Fund for Freedom of Thought, registered in Germany, supports independent, forward-thinking individuals in the Arab world. The fund was established in 1998, the 800th anniversary of the death of the Arab philosopher Ibn Rushd (Averroes) and the 50th anniversary of the UN Declaration of Human Rights. The fund grants awards to individuals who have contributed to freedom and democracy in the Arab world.[9]

CSID, discussed earlier in the report, seeks to bring together secularists and moderate Islamists into networks of Muslim democrats. CSID has partnered with Street Law—a Washington-based NGO that develops curriculum materials and conduct training programs in law, democracy, and human rights—to work with community leaders in Morocco, Algeria, Jordan, and Egypt to develop materials and strategies that show the connection between Islamic and democratic principles. To implement this program, the project has hired local authors to rewrite Street Law's books to place them in a Muslim context.[10]

CSID has organized workshops in a number of Middle East countries, including Jordan, Egypt, Morocco, Tunisia, Nigeria, Turkey, Iran, and Iraq. CISD's approach is to bring together activists of different ideological persuasions and encourage them to seek common ground. As the organization's Web site states, there is no litmus test for participation in CSID activities. CSID works to clarify to what extent Western democratic principles are permissible from an Islamic standpoint. Future CSID projects include developing a directory of Muslim democrats, holding seminars and training workshops for Muslim students in the United States, and providing democratic education and training for Muslim imams in the United States.[11]

---

[9]   Ibn Rushd Fund for Freedom of Thought, "Who Are We?" Web page, n.d.

[10]   RAND discussion with Radwan Masmoudi, Washington, D.C., May 2005.

[11]   See Center for Islam and the Study of Democracy, *2004 President's Report*.

Regional Network-Building Efforts

No regional moderate Muslim networks currently exist in the Middle East, although CSID plans to establish offices in Jordan and Morocco to create a network of Muslim democrats in each country. These national networks could then be combined into a regional network.[12] Moderate (or at least non-Wahhabi) groups have networked through the Tripoli-based *al-Da'wa al-Islamiyya* Society, a Libyan-funded NGO that competes with the Saudi foundations to provide support to Islamic educational, social, and health programs throughout the Muslim world. The society also promotes interfaith dialogue with the Catholic Church and the World Council of Churches.[13]

Democracy Building in Iraq

Iraq represents one of the more extreme cases of the situation found in a number of Arab countries, where decades of authoritarian rule have decimated the civil-society institutions that constitute the building blocs of democracy. Before the overthrow of the Hashemite monarchy in 1958, Iraq had a vibrant civil society, and, if not exactly a democratic political system, the institutions and trappings of parliamentary government. All of this was obliterated in the following 45 years of military and Ba'athist dictatorship, so that after the overthrow of Saddam Hussein the only avenues left for political expression were those parties that had existed outside of Iraq during Hussein's dictatorship, groups with connections to the religious establishment, or ethnically based groups such as the Kurdish political parties.

This is not to say that there is no diversity of political expression in Iraq. In fact, there is probably more political diversity in Iraq than in most Arab countries—outside of the outlawed Ba'ath Party and the violent insurgents and terrorists, all sectors in the political spectrum from Communists to Islamists are now active in Iraqi politics. What

---

[12] RAND discussion with Radwan Masmoudi, Washington, D.C., May 2005.

[13] "Sociedad Mundial del 'Dawa al-Islamiyya,'" Web page, May 2, 2003.

is lacking, at least up to this point, is a center that transcends sectarian and ethnic differences.

Building this center, and with it a normal political process in Iraq, is further complicated by high levels of lawlessness, terrorism, and insurgency that have aggravated the sectarian cleavages within the society. The breakdown of order has made the functioning of civil-society institutions difficult and dangerous; nevertheless, the building blocks of civil society are present in Iraq, which has a substantial middle class and, by the standards of the Arab world, a well-educated population. After the overthrow of Saddam, there was an outpouring of civil society: More than 160 political parties and between 100 and 200 newspapers were established. This flourishing of civil society was cut short by the upsurge in terrorism and violence, but if security and stability could be restored, there could be a rapid and massive expansion of civil society.[14]

Not enough is being done, however, to lay the foundations for secular and liberal civil-society groups. At present, capacity-building programs for Iraqi political parties have focused on the Supreme Council for the Islamic Revolution in Iraq and the Dawa Party, both Islamist organizations with strong links to Iran. Not much is being done to cultivate new political leadership more attuned to liberal democracy.[15]

Strengthening secular and liberal groups will be particularly important in view of the growing influence of the Islamist parties and the language in the Iraqi constitution that declares Islam to be a fundamental source of legislation, guarantees the Islamic identity of the majority of the Iraqi people, and states that no law can contradict "the undisputed rules of Islam." In order to ensure that laws are consistent with Islamic principles, the constitution provides for the appointment of experts in Islamic law to the Supreme Court by a two-thirds vote of Parliament.

Despite the undoubted progress registered over the past two years in launching and sustaining a democratic political process in Iraq, non-

---

[14] RAND discussion with Radwan Masmoudi, Washington, D.C., November 2005.

[15] RAND discussion with staff of U.S. Commission on International Religious Freedom, Washington, D.C., November 2005.

Muslim religious minorities and women's rights groups are under severe pressure and are afraid of the future. Non-Muslims and women's rights advocates fear that human rights provisions in the Constitution would be undermined by judges interpreting the law in accordance with Islamic precepts. There is also concern that the provision that guarantees the Islamic identity of the majority may permit the criminalization of apostasy, blasphemy, and other crimes under Islamic law.[16] Strengthening the forces countervailing the Islamists will be critical in ensuring the democratic and pluralistic character of the new Iraq.

---

[16] RAND discussion with staff of U.S. Commission on International Religious Freedom, Washington, D.C., October 2005.

CHAPTER NINE

Secular Muslims: A Forgotten Dimension in the War of Ideas

When Western experts discuss the ongoing war of ideas in the Islamic world—the ideological struggle between Islamism and proponents of modernity and moderation—they tend to assume that secular Muslims are not serious contenders. This stems from a widespread belief that Muslim society is too deeply shaped by religion to be amenable to a purely secular philosophy at this time, and, further, that the relationship between religion and politics in Islam is so inherently different from that in the West that the ideas of the separation of church and state and of faith as a private and individual matter are not culturally transferable. Any secular Muslims that do exist in the Middle East or the diaspora are assumed to be peripheral figures having no real influence or appeal. This dismissal is so pervasive that it is hard to find any public diplomacy focused toward Muslim secularism and its adherents.

Before turning to the specific question of secularism and Islam, a few general remarks about terminology should be made. What we can broadly include under the heading of secularism consists, in the historical context as well as in the current debate, of several distinct but related strands.

Political secularism advocates the separation of religion and the state, with the state viewed by liberal secularists as the neutral administrator of daily life and governance and the source of a worldly rule of law. *Liberal secularism* treats religion as a personal spiritual matter or, in some instances, as a communal matter (but one that must be kept discrete from the political realm). *Authoritarian secularism*, manifested in the ruling parties of Syria, Egypt, and Tunisia, for example, subordinates religion as well as other social institutions to the purposes of the state and the ruling party.[1] When we speak of Muslim secularists as potential partners in a network-building initiative we refer, of course, to liberal secularists. Authoritarian secularists not only have goals at cross-purposes with the values we want to promote, but often have strategic interests in common with Islamists. (Take, for instance, the case of the Egyptian government and the Muslim Brotherhood. The main victim of political repression in Egypt has not been the Brotherhood, but liberal Muslim opposition sectors.)

Although earlier RAND work on this topic questioned the premise that secularism was broadly unacceptable to Islamic societies, its role was only touched upon briefly. We observed that in purely ideological terms, liberal secularists were among the most compatible with Western political and social values. We also noted that "secular regimes have managed to hold power, legitimacy, and even popularity, and secular movements have gained huge followings. One of the Islamic world's more successful states, Turkey, achieved its progress through a policy of aggressive secularism." Finally, we observed that liberal Muslim secularists not only were underfunded and lacking a platform competitive with those of the Islamists, but were also viewed with suspicion by Western governments, which had two principal objections to supporting these groups: the belief that secularists did not command support in the Muslim world and concern over their links to leftist and anti-American sectors.[2] We did not at that time conduct a more serious inquiry into the nature, effectiveness, and background of secularists or secularism in the Muslim world.

Nor did we intend to do so in the current project. Secular Muslims were initially included primarily in the spirit of due diligence, because we wanted to be comprehensive in our review of their potential. We did not expect secular Muslims to be a significant force. Rather, we

---

[1]   See Angel Rabasa et al., 2004.

[2]   Benard, 2003, p. 25. In countries such as Bahrain, liberals see the Islamists as the primary threat and cooperate with leftist and ex-Communist political sectors.

presumed that moderates and liberal Muslims would populate the bulk of our study. What we found instead was that none of the prevailing assumptions stand up to scrutiny. Secularism is not inherent in the West.[3] It is not absent, incompatible, or foreign to Islam. And secularists are not a new and negligible phenomenon in the Middle East.

We discovered that the prevailing assumption concerning the irrelevance of secularism in the Islamic context is more stereotype than fact. Historically and intellectually, the role of secularism in the Islamic tradition is considerably more significant than analysts and policymakers generally believe. Further, secularism in today's Muslim world seems to be in an incipient period of growth, with an evolving group of leaders and an expanding network. A core of writers and thinkers has recently emerged, and they are providing each other with platforms and support, aided by like-minded liberal groups in the West. In doing so, they build on a twofold tradition: on the deep strands of rationalist and humanist thought present historically in Islamic thinking and philosophy, and on the secularist movements of the last century.

Secularism can be a risky posture for a Muslim, whether practicing, nonpracticing, or having openly or de facto left the faith—the last

---

[3] Some historians argue that rationalism, critical thinking, and scientific inquiry—the cornerstones of Western scientific advancement and of secularism, in other words—were brought to the West by the Islamic East, transmitted from the ancient Greeks. (John Hobson, *The Eastern Origins of Western Civilization*, Cambridge, UK: Cambridge University Press, 2004.) Certainly, the ninth century saw a number of rationalist philosophers, scientists, and professionals attain influence and prominence in the Muslim world. Best known are the Persian physician Zakaria al-Razi, who has been classified by historians as a freethinker and who conducted his medical research in a spirit of empiricism. The philosopher Abu Nasr al-Farabi built upon Plato's and Aristotle's writings on epistemology and on rightful governance. Born in Turkestan and educated in Baghdad, his posture is perhaps best classified as humanist, with his best known political publication, *The Virtuous City*, describing the ideal polity as one in which the inhabitants cooperate with each other in the interest of general happiness. Another ninth-century intellectual, al-Kindi, was active as a mathematician and physician; he published nearly 250 books on the natural sciences, music, and philosophy. A major Baghdad hospital is named after al-Kindi, who famously pronounced, "We ought not to be embarrassed of appreciating the truth and of obtaining it wherever it comes from, even if it comes from races distant and nations different from us. Nothing should be dearer to the seeker of truth than the truth itself, and there is no deterioration of the truth, nor (should there be any) belittling of one who speaks it or conveys it." (Islamic Philosophy Online, "al-Kindi Site," Web page, n.d.

status not even acknowledged as a permissible option by conservative and fundamentalist Muslims.[4] To turn away from or even to criticize certain core aspects of Islam is, of course, considered apostasy by most Islamists, an offense for which death is the appropriate punishment. The controversial postures—which can create a situation of personal danger for any individual who endorses them—include any direct criticism of the literal and unchanging truth of the Quran and of Islam, the belief that it should be permissible to leave Islam and to profess atheism or agnosticism or to adopt a different religion, and, in some countries, professing that Islam should be relegated to the private sphere and that civil law should override *shari'a*.

Some secularist dissidents operate under pseudonyms and avoid public appearances. One of the most prominent examples is the author, writing under the pseudonym Ibn Warraq, of *Why I Am Not a Muslim* and, more recently, *Leaving Islam: Apostates Speak Out*.[5] Ibn Warraq is also associated with a number of secularist initiatives, including the Institute for the Secularization of Islamic Society, of which he is a founder.

Others speak out in public, persisting even when threats are issued against them. This group includes such high-profile political activists as the Somali-born former Dutch parliamentarian Ayaan Hirsi Ali. The killing of her collaborator Theo Van Gogh and the credible death threats against her, which have required her to frequently change addresses and retain permanent bodyguards, have deterred her neither from continuing her criticism of Islam nor from her intention of filming the planned second segment of the very documentary that had so outraged Van Gogh's killer.

Syrian-American Wafa Sultan was certainly aware of the potential consequences of her words when she made statements on *al-Jazeera* television that were unequivocally critical not just of fundamentalism

---

[4]   The influential Salafi cleric Yussuf al-Qaradawi denounces secularism in the strongest possible terms as a stance that can lead to the destruction of Islam. Yusef al-Qaradawi, "Secularism vs. Islam," Web page, n.d.

[5]   Ibn Warraq, *Why I Am Not a Muslim*, Amherst, N.Y.: Prometheus, 1995; and Ibn Warraq, *Leaving Islam: Apostates Speak Out*, Amherst, N.Y.: Prometheus, 2003.

but of Islam. To say, as she does, that she is "questioning every single teaching of our holy book" and to urge an adoption of Western values and Western culture were bound to inspire exactly what followed—accusations of apostasy and death threats, along with sudden fame and a vastly expanded audience for her views.[6]

Aside from personal risk, secular Muslims also face a number of additional obstacles:

- Secularism has been associated, especially in the Arab world, with failed authoritarian political systems.
- Secularism has often been connected with leftist ideas, individuals, and groups, which can cause it to be rejected, especially in the United States, by official programs and agencies that are otherwise heavily engaged in fostering, funding, and promoting a discourse on Islamic reform.
- Secularism is often confused with atheism, especially by Muslim and Middle Eastern audiences; its opponents do much to encourage this confusion. While opinions about the relationship between state and religion (and even the relationship between mullahs or other religious authorities and the individual believer) are not nearly as uniform as is sometimes assumed, and while even traditional publics can in many cases well tolerate (and even welcome) the notion that religion is a personal, family, and community matter that should remain separate from politics, public life, and the state, atheism is much less acceptable.

On the positive side of the ledger, the secularist position is classically liberal. Unlike Islamists, there is little danger that secularists are in fact pursuing a hidden agenda to undermine liberal democracy. Since liberal secularists do not advocate violence and support religious toleration, they should be able to find a foothold in the mainstream along with liberal and moderate Muslims. Their participation would strengthen moderate coalitions, and their commitment to the separation of reli-

---

6   John Brody, "For Muslim Who Says Violence Destroys Islam, Violent Threats," *New York Times*, March 11, 2006.

gion and state makes them less likely to form alliances of convenience with Islamists or to tolerate efforts to subordinate politics to religion.

In the current Islamic debate, we can identify a clear group of scholars and writers who are assuming a strongly rationalist stance while either rejecting secularism (perhaps for tactical reasons, because they think embracing it will make them less effective, or because they feel it too personally dangerous) or skirting the issue. Nonsecular rationalists assert the right (and indeed the responsibility) of the individual to analyze the text of the Quran and obtain his or her own understanding of its meaning and application.

For an example of this line of argument we turn to the modernist Syrian writer Muhammad Shahrour.[7] Secularist groups in the Islamic world, he argues, generally wanted not a separation of religion from governance, but the suppression of religion altogether. Largely comprised of Marxists and Communists (along with some Arab nationalists), these groups were problematic on two scores. First, they were intolerant and repressive, replacing the dominance of religion with a "state monopoly on truth." Second, they failed to deliver on their promise to modernize society.[8] Shahrour's independent reading brings him, as he explains, to a number of conclusions that run counter to fundamentalism; in several basic points, Shahrour's thinking also runs counter to the mainstream orthodox Muslim view. He believes, for instance, that the Quran does not mandate the death sentence for any offenses and that the term jihad is not applicable to any circumstances that apply today. He departs from orthodoxy in his dismissal of other religious sources (including the *sunna*), his downgrading of the Prophet to nothing more than an exceptionally admirable but flawed human being, and his disregard of all intervening religious scholarship.[9]

---

[7] The examples that follow are intended to be illustrative, not comprehensive or representative. It would be advisable in future research to create a systematic overview of the secularist presence in the Muslim world.

[8] Muhammad Shahrour, "The Divine Text and Pluralism in Muslim Societies," *Muslim Political Report*, No. 14, July/August 1997.

[9] Shahrour, 1997.

Ali Ahmad Sa'id (better known under the pen name Adonis) is a poet with a long history of political engagement. After serving a prison sentence for activism in his native Syria, Adonis moved to Lebanon and thereafter to France. He is a decided secularist as well as a rationalist. He believes that "religion [should] become a personal and spiritual experience" and that "all issues pertaining to civil and human affairs must be left up to the law and to the people." A religious state is unacceptable to Adonis, even if it is the outcome of a democratic election. He reveals a personal aversion to religion, which he sees as a product of a fear of freedom and responsibility—part of the same psychology that leads people to flock to dictators and accept authoritarian rule. However, Adonis also believes that as a personal matter religious beliefs must be afforded respect.[10] Again, the acceptability—let alone the popularity—of such a view is difficult to determine.

Egyptian scholar and professor Nasr Abu Zayd was put on trial in Egypt in 1995 for stating that he regarded the Quran as a work of literature and a text that should be subjected to rational and scholarly analysis. Found guilty, he was ordered to divorce his wife, who as a Muslim could not be permitted to remain married to a heretic. The couple obtained asylum in the Netherlands, and Abu Zayd is now a professor at the Universities of Leiden and Utrecht, where he writes, teaches, and makes frequent public appearances.

Asghar Ali Engineer, a prominent representative of Indian Islamic secularism, has repeatedly been the target of physical attacks by gangs of fundamentalist thugs. He has also been arrested on dubious charges manufactured by his opponents and quickly dismissed by the courts. On one such occasion in 2000, Engineer's supporters initiated an international campaign highlighting his detention. Engineer is a recipient of the Swedish Rightful Living Foundation's "Alternative Nobel Prize," which is awarded by the Speaker of the Swedish Parliament.

---

[10] Middle East Media Research Insitute, "Renowned Syrian Poet Adonis: The Arabs Are Extinct Like the Sumerians, Greeks and Pharaohs; If the Arabs Are So Inept They Cannot Be Democratic, External Intervention Will Not Make Them So," excerpts from an interview with Adonis (aka Ali Ahmad Sa'id) on Dubai TV, March 11, 2006, translated, *Middle East Media Research Institute Special Dispatch Series*, No. 1121, March 21, 2006.

Younus Shaikh is a Pakistani physician who was jailed in 2000 on blasphemy charges. The charges centered on his statements that Muhammad's parents could not have been Muslims, since Islam had not yet been revealed during their lifetime, and that Muhammad was not a Muslim before receiving his first revelation. In 2001, Shaikh received the death sentence from a Pakistani court. Following persistent interventions from liberal and human-rights groups and Western governments, he was released from prison a year later and allowed to seek refuge in Switzerland.[11]

The popular Lebanese musician Marcel Khalife was tried in a Lebanese court for blasphemy on two separate occasions, most recently in 1999, merely for placing part of a Quranic *sura* into one of his songs, although there was no critical context or message attached. He was ultimately acquitted. However, Khalife's arrest sparked a strong debate in the region and within the diaspora, where he has many fans.[12]

Secular Muslim Organizations

On the organizational side, we can distinguish three relevant groupings of secular Muslim organizations. First are institutions solely devoted to the promotion of a secular Islam; second are institutions that are dedicated to secularism, rationalism, or humanism more broadly and that devote—in many cases as a recent addition—a separate section of their platform to Islam; third are liberal institutions that affiliate themselves with the Islamic secularist undertaking by endorsing or supporting it in some fashion, for example through financial help, by inviting or giving awards to secular Muslims, or by using their own Web site to spread the message of secularism.[13]

---

[11] For details on the circumstances of his three-year imprisonment and ultimate release, see International Humanist and Ethical Union, "Younis Sheik Free," Web page, January 23, 2004.

[12] Joe Lockard, "Marcel Khalife and Blasphemy," *Bad Subjects*, Web site, December 19, 1999.

[13] The following list is illustrative, not comprehensive. It relies on the self-descriptions of these organizations, which the scope of this project did not allow us to further investigate.

Institutions Solely Devoted to the Promotion of a Secular Islam

The Free Muslims' Coalition describes itself as having twelve chapters in the United States, one in Canada, and two in Egypt. It was founded by Kamal Nawash, a Palestinian immigrant and lawyer who has been the legal director of the American-Arab Anti-Discrimination Committee and who was a Republican candidate for the Virginia State Senate in 2003.[14]

The Progressive Muslim Union has a youthful governing board with strong elements of pop culture and an affiliation with the modernist Web site *MuslimWakeUp*. Its "Statements of Principle" clearly endorse secularism.[15]

The Institute of Islamic Studies was founded in India in 1980 by Asghar Ali Engineer and has its offices in Mumbai. In its self-description, it explains that it intends to serve "reformist ends and was set up by those who felt the need for rethinking issues in Islam." The

---

[14] The statement on secularism on the organization's Web site is worth citing in its entirety: "The Coalition supports the right of all peoples to self government, but recognizes the importance of a solid system of government which guarantees a secular democracy protecting the rights of all people, regardless of gender, race or religion, and strives tirelessly to eliminate threats to democracy including extremism and terrorism. The Coalition fosters this secular environment by opening debates on the prerequisite of secularism in governments in the Middle East & North Africa, rallying against Islamist propaganda in media outlets, in institutions of education and in political campaigns, and by exploring the creation of secular democracy-preserving constitutions for Arab and Muslim countries. The Coalition believes that Muslims must be reeducated about the benefits of secularism and that the failure of their governments to bring them peace and prosperity was not because they were secular. The Coalition also believes that democracy can not succeed unless terrorism is defeated and Islamic extremism is discredited."

[15] Points ten and eleven state: "We endorse the separation of religion and state in all matters of public policy, not only in North America, but also across the Muslim world. We believe that secular government is the only way to achieve the Islamic ideal of freedom from compulsion in matters of faith and that the separation of religion and state is a necessary prerequisite to building democratic societies, where religious, ethnic, and racial minorities are accepted as equal citizens enjoying full dignity and human rights enunciated in the 1948 UN Declaration of Universal Human Rights. We recognize the growing danger of religious extremism and view the politicization of religion and the intrusion of religion into politics as twin threats to civil society and humane civilization. We vow to resist the intrusion of religion into politics and the exploitation of religion for political ends." Progressive Muslim Union, "PMU Statement of Principles," Web page, n.d.

catalyst for the establishment of the institute was the Islamic revolution in Iran and the two consequences of that event that concerned the founders: a newly arisen Western concern about political Islam (and the possible attendant measures the West might take) and the upsurge in fundamentalist thinking and influence. In the face of these looming external and internal threats, the group hoped their new organization would encourage a rethinking and modernization of Islam.

The Centre for the Study of Society and Secularism, also in Mumbai, is a later offshoot of the Institute of Islamic Studies. Founded by a group of Indian intellectuals in 1993, it goes a step beyond the Institute to clearly advocate secularism as the only effective bulwark against the threat of "growing communalism" and the only basis for "a cohesive society."[16] The center publishes the quarterly *Indian Journal of Secularism* along with a large number of studies and books. Its activities include research, field studies, workshops and seminars, along with more populist outreach activities such as street plays (a common medium of civic education in the region) and youth camps.

Rationalist/Humanist Organizations That Support Muslim Secularism

The Giordano Bruno Foundation is named after the 16th century philosopher executed as a heretic in Rome. It is located in Mastershausen, Germany (near Mainz), where it inhabits a spacious building and hosts events and conferences. The foundation awarded a prize to Necla Kelek, a high-profile Turkish-German sociologist who advocates assimilation and secularism, argues for stringent citizenship tests for naturalized Muslim immigrants, and has demanded harsher penalties for "culture crimes" such as forced marriages and honor killings.

The Center for Inquiry West (online at www.cfiwest.org) and the Center for Inquiry Transnational are based in Hollywood, California, and were founded by Paul Kurtz (as was the Council for Secular Humanism in New York). The centers' journal *Free Inquiry* devotes extensive space to critiques of Islam and Islamism and to the notion of Islamic secularism. The organizations' leaders believe that Iran, where

---

[16] Centre for the Study of Society and Secularism, "About Us," Web page, n.d.

clerical rule has created a significant backlash against political Islam, is a promising location for the expansion of secularist values. Their subsidiary Farsi-language Web site, New Horizons, has the declared aim of spreading the values of secularism to Iran and Iranians. That project is headed by Armen Saginian, who also advances this agenda through a radio and a television station broadcasting to Iran.

The National Secular Society is a British organization originally founded in 1866 by MP Charles Bradlaugh. It was instrumental in the narrow defeat of the "Incitement to Religious Hatred" amendment to the Racial and Religious Hatred Act 2006 in the British Parliament—an amendment secularists feared would limit freedom of expression and the right to criticize religions.

Rationalist International is a multinational group of intellectuals and activists representing a range of cultures and religions. Younus Shaikh is at the forefront of the Muslim presence in this organization.

Online Platforms

Examples of Internet platforms for the expression of secularist views include the popular www.annaqed.com. (*Annaqed* means "the critic" in Arabic, and the Web site's symbol is a Hyde Park–style lectern from behind which an agitated man declaims his views.) The Web site was originally intended as a forum for Arabic-speaking residents of the United States. It has since added an English language section, and the Arab section is thought to be popular in the Middle East.

Middle East Transparent (www.metransparent.com) is online in Arabic, English, and French. While not explicitly secularist, it provides a place for liberal thinkers and intellectuals from the region to publicize their views. It also publishes articles and papers by Western analysts and academics.

www.free-minds.org is a Saudi-based site with a somewhat eccentric slant. Introducing itself as a pious mainstream Islamic grouping dedicated to *da'wa*, it then proceeds to list as the correct orthodox Islamic positions on social rights, women's status, interfaith relations, and *shari'a* criminal punishments stances which in fact represent a cutting-edge, progressive posture bordering on what actual orthodox Muslims would probably consider heresy. For example, the Web site challenges the five pillars of the faith and claims that the first of them, the *shahada* (or declaration of faith), is based on an unreliable *hadith* and should not be followed.[17] The Web site includes a map of the world which, when the visitor clicks on a respective region, lists the members resident there.

www.qantara.de is a Web site funded by the German government as part of its MEPI-like Middle Eastern outreach effort. This Web site does not take overt positions; it is a discussion forum where conservative views are also represented (for instance in debates over the *hijab*). It is, however, liberal in its intent to foster a culture of spirited debate, and liberal and secularist voices are given significant room. For example, the argument in favor of the separation of religion and state made by the Grand Mufti of Marseille in an interview with the Indonesian Liberal Islam Network is reprinted on this Web site.

www.nosharia.com is a Canada-based Web site online in Arabic, Farsi, Kurdish, English, French, and German. It was started in response to one particular issue: the push to allow Muslims in Canada to establish *shari'a* courts for certain kinds of legal matters. The Web site became a rallying ground for opponents of the measure, who argued that it undermined crucial principles of Western democracy and placed immigrant women in an untenable position.[18] Ultimately 87 organizations from 14 countries banded together to oppose the Canadian initiative. The Web site has since expanded to become a broader platform for civil rights and secularism.

---

[17] free-minds.org, "The Shahada," Web page, n.d.

[18] *Shari'a* courts were theoretically a voluntary option but, in fact, family and community pressure would generally make it difficult if not impossible for a Muslim woman to choose a secular court, even though her legal standing in those courts would be superior relative to a shari'a court.

Notable Muslim Secularist Figures and Their Views

Soheib Bencheikh, the Grand Mufti of Marseille, publicly supports not only the French headscarf ban, but more broadly, the principles of secularism and laicism (terms he uses interchangeably). Bencheikh defines secularism as "administrative neutrality," by which he means that the state should perform the tasks of governance in separation from religion. In an interview, he states that "the separation between religion and politics will clarify Islam as a divine spiritual doctrine, not as an instrument which can be misused to gain the power." This, he argues, was the original nature of Islam. "Assimilation between religion and politics in Islam is a new phenomenon," he says, and one which is "hazardous to Islam." He cites the Muslim Brotherhood of Egypt as one of the principal originators of this wrong turn.[19]

Shaker al-Nabulsi, a Jordanian professor now living in the United States, is the author of the "Manifesto of New Arab Liberals," which among other things proposes that "the prevailing sacred values, traditions, legislations, and moral values (should be subjected to) in-depth scrutiny."[20] This is a classically rationalist statement, as is his insistence that the *shari'a* laws can only be understood within the context of the period in history during which they were developed, and thus are not eternally valid.[21] He has also been involved in the petition to hold radical clerics who support violence accountable for terrorist incidents.[22]

The Kuwaiti professor Ahmad al-Baghdadi has been in trouble with the courts repeatedly, receiving sentences for such diverse offenses

---

[19] Soheib Bencheikh, "Islam and Secularism," interview by Liberal Islam Network, April 2004.

[20] Meneham Milson, "Reform vs. Islamism in the Arab World Today," Middle East Media Research Institute Special Report No. 34, September 15, 2004.

[21] For an example, see Shaker Al-Nabulsi, "Arab Progressive: The Arabs Are Still Slaves to a Medieval Mentality," excerpts from an article published on www.rezgar.com, August 14, 2004, Middle East Research Institute Special Dispatch Series No. 786, September 20, 2004.

[22] The Middle East Media Research Institute Reform Project includes a number of other reformers who hold rationalist, humanist, or secularist views, such as the Saudi Mansur Al-Nuqeidan and the Egyptian Gamal al-Bana.

as expressing his view that the Prophet failed to convert some of the people to whom he preached, saying that he would prefer for his son to study music rather than the Quran, and implying a connection between Quranic studies, intellectual backwardness, and terrorism.[23] He continues to express secularist and rationalist views in some of the most direct language we encountered in our survey. For example, al-Baghdadi wrote an article praising Western Orientalist scholars whose works today are more commonly viewed as politically incorrect for producing levels of scholarship, analysis, and documentation incomparably more rigorous than that of their Arab contemporaries. He has also published articles in the Kuwaiti media in which he aggressively argues for the necessity of secularism.[24]

Tarek Heggy is a former Egyptian business executive and vice president of regional Shell Oil. Since leaving Shell he has become a prolific writer and lecturer on political, social, and cultural reform. In one of the Doha Debates, he was pitted against former Malaysian Prime Minister Mahathir in a debate on the topic "This House Believes in the Separation of Mosque and State."[25] In that debate, Heggy argued that religion could provide an overarching framework of ethical values but should not be involved in practical governance, legislation, administration, or even a determination of how those principles were to be implemented in daily life.[26]

---

[23] A. Dankowitz, "Arab Intellectuals: Under Threat by Islamists," Middle East Media Research Institute Inquiry and Analysis Series No. 254, November 23, 2005; Human Rights Watch, "Imprisoned Kuwaiti Scholar: Academics Demand Release," press release, October 13, 1999.

[24] Ahmad al-Baghdadi, "Kuwati Progressive Scholar: 'All the Good Is in Secular Thought, All the Evil in Religious Thought,'" translated excerpts from articles appearing in the November 14, 2004, and November 16–17, 2004, editions of *Al-Siyassa*, Middle East Media Research Initiative Special Dispatch No. 823, December 3, 2004.

[25] Tarek Heggy, "This House Believes in the Separation of Mosque and State," transcript of comments made during debate, Doha Debates, November 30, 2004.

[26] This is reflected in the response he sent to a fundamentalist who had been barraging him with religious materials in an effort to bring him back into the fold: "I am a person who believes that progress is the yield of science and management . . . . Religion will not bridge the very huge gap between us and the advanced world. Frankly, I am a son of Western civilization: I adore and value everything that comes from the West . . . .I believe that we (the

Canadian-Iranian Homa Arjomand is a founder of the campaign against *shari'a* courts in Canada and a frequent speaker in Europe and in the media. Another of her campaigns seeks to ban Islamic religious schools in the West, arguing that "political Islam, as a reactionary, anti-human . . . movement" plays a divisive and radicalizing role.[27] The petition further asserts that children under the age of 16 should not be exposed to any religious influence, because they are not mature enough to judge its message. Arjomand received the Toronto Humanist of the Year award for 2006.

Somali born Ayaan Hirsi Ali is a former Member of Parliament in the Netherlands and a well known public representative of the values of secularism and of the universality of civic freedom, rule of law, and women's and human rights beyond multiculturalist relativism. She is a declared atheist and open critic of aspects of the life of the Prophet Muhammad and of the negative treatment of women in Islam, which she believes flows from basic Islamic doctrinal principles. She testified against the introduction of *shari'a* courts in Canada. A large number of liberal organizations have honored her activism: She received the Freedom Prize of the Danish Liberal Party (2004) and the Democratic Prize of the Liberal Party of Sweden (2005), was named one of the most influential persons of 2005 by *Time* magazine, and was chosen as the "European of the Year" by the editors of the European edition of *Readers' Digest* in 2006.[28]

Arabic speaking and Muslim people) live in the 11th and not the 21st century. I do not hate America . . . I do not hate Christians . . . I do not hate Jews . . . but I hate BACKWARD-NESS . . . .I respect everybody's right to believe in whatever he/she opts to believe in. But for me, the values of democracy, human and women's rights, otherness, universality of science and knowledge, cultural and religious tolerance, are the values that I belong to." Excerpt from a correspondence between Heggy and Amal, a Saudi fundamentalist, on April 10, 2006, quoted by permission of Tarek Heggy, April 11, 2006.

[27] Homa Arjomand, "International Declaration, Islamic Schools Should Be Banned, Children Have No Religion," petition, n.d.

[28] *Wikipedia*, s.v. "Ayaan Hirsi Ali."

Manifestos and Position Papers

In the spring of 2006, a group of anti-Islamist, primarily secular intellectuals issued a manifesto condemning Islamism as the contemporary form of totalitarianism (see Appendix B) and calling for the promotion of "secular values for all" and for the triumph of the "critical spirit" and of "Enlightenment." The twelve signatories included prominent members of the anti-totalitarian and anti-Islamist cultural elite: Ayaan Hirsi Ali; Salman Rushdie, who was famously the target of a fatwa and was obliged to spend many years in hiding subsequent to the publication of his novel *The Satanic Verses*; Taslima Nasreen, similarly the subject of several fatwas and calls for her execution in her native Bangladesh for protesting the mistreatment of Hindus and calling for the revision of the Quran; Irshad Manji, one of the more outspoken contemporary critics of Islam and author of *The Trouble with Islam Today*; and Mehdi Mozaffari, an Iranian living in exile in Denmark and author of *Fatwa: Violence and Discourtesy*, a study of fatwas.[29] The other Middle Eastern signatories—Chahla Chafiq, Maryam Namazie, and Antoine Sfeir—are also intellectuals and authors of books critiquing Islam. The manifesto's European signatories are left-leaning intellectuals such as Philippe Val, director of the leftist French newspaper *Charlie Hebdo*; anti-fascist French philosopher Bernard-Henri Levy; and Caroline Fourest, a proponent of laicism.

The Iranian Secularist Society is a small group based in the UK, and at least some of its members are associated with the Iranian Communist Party.[30] The society published a manifesto stating that religion should be kept separate from politics, should not receive public funds, should not play a role in the education system, and should be prevented from interfering with civil liberties.

There is an emerging transnational network of laicist and secularist individuals, groups, and movements. This strand of thinking also

---

[29] Mehdi Mozaffari, *Fatwa: Violence and Discourtesy*, Aarhus, Denmark: Aarhus University Press, July 1998.

[30] Maryam Namazie, for instance, includes a function in that party in her biography. Maryam Namazie, "Biography," Web page, n.d.

has a popular dimension. We see this in the emerging Muslim-diaspora comedians of Middle Eastern descent, some of whom have acquired large followings based on their routines mocking fundamentalism and critical of Islam. These individuals also face death threats and intimidation, but conversely are popular role models in the more secular-minded segments of the immigrant community. Emerging autonomously, they are a particularly interesting expression of what we might term a grassroots assimilationist secularism.

In Norway, for example, comedienne Shabana Rehman, originally from Pakistan, likes to appear onstage in a burqa, which she removes to reveal a red cocktail dress before launching into her monologue against *shari'a* law; she espouses the benefits of integration into Western modernity. Her message, delivered in a very different medium, echoes the modern secular Western mindset. Rehman appears frequently on Western European television and radio and writes a popular newspaper column. In addition to secularism and modernity, she also conveys the benefits of integration, urging fellow immigrants to appreciate the freedoms and opportunities of life in the West.[31] She has also led political protests against honor killings, forced marriages, and the inclination of Western governments to tolerate human rights abuses in their minority communities under the guise of multiculturalism. These are the same issues that mobilized Hirsi Ali and that inspire other outspoken diaspora reformers. Turkish-German author Necla Kelek is another example.

In addition to a limited (but not negligible) number of secularist groups and individuals who achieve notoriety and prominence in the Middle East and the broader Muslim world, there are the uncounted numbers who stand up for such principles in their immediate environment. There is certainly a much larger number who sympathize with these views, or at least find them worthy of thoughtful consideration.

Within the first category we must include the Saudi teachers who lost their jobs and faced blasphemy charges for such classically ratio-

---

[31] For more on Shabana Rehman visit her Web site. See also, Sarah Coleman, "Shabana Rehman, Making Fun of the Mullahs," *World Press Review*, Vol. 9, No. 50, September 2003.

nalist stances as encouraging their students to apply critical thinking to resolve contradictions in the text of the Quran.[32] This group also includes a significant number of journalists arrested on similar charges, such as the Afghan magazine editor who was put on trial for blasphemy in 2005 because he wrote that it was permissible to leave the religion of Islam.[33]

To what extent do these views (or at least these discussions) resonate, and with which portion of the public? This question is well worth a more systematic analysis, which has not taken place thus far due to preconceived assumptions about the values and attitudes of Muslim publics.

We note, for example, that the blogging scene is replete with secular notions, though not all bloggers expressly place their thoughts in the secularist tradition (or even seem aware of it). For example, some Gulf bloggers give voice to a spontaneous kind of rationalist or secularist sentiment when they ruminate about the problems facing their countries and societies and arrive at strongly stated doubts about the connection between Islam, the state, and the absence in much of the Muslim world of the freedom of an individual to decide the nature and degree of his or her own religiosity.[34]

---

[32] Human Rights Watch, "Saudi Arabia: Teachers Silenced on Blasphemy Charges," *Human Rights News*, November 17, 2005.

[33] "Editor's Arrest on Blasphemy Charges Highlights Difficulties Facing Journalists," *Pak-Tribune Online*, October 23, 2005.

[34] This is further explored in Cheryl Benard, *Freedom Bytes: The Internet and the War of Ideas*, Santa Monica, Calif.: RAND Corporation, WR-370-SR, forthcoming.

CHAPTER TEN

Conclusions and Recommendations

Applying the Lessons of the Cold War

The network-building activities of the United States and Britain during the Cold War provide a number of valuable lessons for today's struggle with radical Islam. This is true at both the strategic and the tactical level, despite the important differences between the two eras outlined in Chapter Three.

On the strategic level, the United States understood at the beginning of the Cold War that network building was a vital part of its overall strategy. Substantial resources were devoted to funding a host of organizations that could compete with Communist-dominated organizations in Western Europe and the Third World. Policymakers also understood their tactical network-building efforts would only succeed if closely tied in to a well thought through strategy guiding U.S. policy across agencies and programs.

The President's Freedom Agenda is the closest approximation to a U.S. grand strategy in the Global War on Terrorism, but this strategy is not linked directly to scattered U.S.-supported efforts to build moderate Muslim networks and institutions. Furthermore, the resources devoted to network-building activities thus far have been minimal in comparison to the resources spent on military and public diplomacy activities. If the United States is truly seeking to influence the outcome of the war of ideas raging in the Muslim world, then it needs to make a commitment, as it did during the Cold War, to support and organize its natural allies.

Another strategy of the United States during the Cold War was to create a networking effort that, while largely defensive, had an offensive component. This meant that although much of the effort was directed at stabilizing and bolstering democratic forces in Western Europe (and later in Asia and the Middle East), there were also efforts to undermine Communist rule in the Soviet bloc through political and information warfare. Our proposal to foster moderate Muslim networks is also largely defensive in nature, since we propose to bolster the capabilities of moderate Muslims resisting the spread of extremist ideologies; however, we also view democracy-promotion efforts that directly confront authoritarian political systems as an essential piece of the larger strategy. The West's efforts to reach out to the peoples of Eastern Europe and the Soviet Union during the Cold War may have a counterpart today in support for democratization in Iran. Of course, Iran, like the old Soviet bloc, is a much more difficult environment for dissident networks to develop in and would require a different strategy from that outlined in this study.

Even more applicable to challenges today are some of the tactical and operational network-building methods employed by the West during the Cold War. One of the key problems the United States faces today is how to maintain the credibility of groups that receive support from the United States or other international bodies. One way to do this is to link the public and private sectors by encouraging well-regarded NGOs to expand their activities in the Muslim world. During the Cold War, organizations ranging from student groups on college campuses to the American Federation of Labor were willing to engage in campaigns to build free and democratic institutions. The role of the U.S. government was to provide operational and financial support that allowed these groups to expand their operations internationally. Today, with many groups and individuals in the United States and Europe organizing themselves to combat Islamist extremism, there should be no shortage of partners for the United States.

In some cases, the U.S. government may have to take a somewhat more active role in forming networks. The highly successful Cold War–era Congress of Cultural Freedom provides an excellent example of how to turn scattered groups of like-minded individuals into a powerful international network with limited U.S. organizational and financial support. The United States would be wise to take a lesson from the Cold War playbook and quietly assist moderate Muslim intellectuals in organizing their own Congress of Freedom to combat radical Islam. The goal would be to construct a permanent, multinational organization that could serve as an intellectual platform for democratic renewal in the Muslim world.

In this project, after reviewing the strategies that were most effective in building a strong and credible body of alternate values, influential dissidents, and reliable counterparts during the Cold War, we surveyed the Muslim world's intellectual, organizational, and ideational makeup. In parallel, we evaluated the U.S. government's current public diplomacy effort as it seeks to reshape political discourse in the Middle East. From this research, we developed a direct implementation path that is described below.

Strategic and Institutional Steps

The first step is for the U.S. government and its allies to make a clear decision to build moderate networks and to create an explicit link between network-building activities and overall U.S. strategy and programs. To achieve this goal, it is necessary to create an institutional structure within the U.S. government to guide, support, oversee, and continuously monitor the effort. Within the framework of this structure, the U.S. government must build up the necessary expertise and capacity to execute the strategy, which includes

1. An ever-evolving and ever-sharpening set of criteria that distinguishes true moderates from opportunists and from extremists camouflaged as moderates, and liberal secularists from authoritarian secularists. The U.S. government needs to have the ability to make situational decisions to *knowingly* and for tactical reasons (i.e., not out of ignorance, or without due and careful consideration) support individuals outside of that range under specific circumstances.

2. An international database of partners (individuals, groups, organizations, institutions, parties, etc.).
3. Mechanisms for monitoring and refining programs, projects, and decisions. These should include a feedback loop to allow for inputs and corrections from those partners who have been found to be most trustworthy.

The network-building effort could initially focus on a core group of reliable partners whose ideological orientation is known, and work outward from there (i.e., following the methodology of underground organizations).

Our approach calls for a few fundamental changes to the current, symmetric strategy of engagement with the Muslim world. The current approach identifies the problem area as the Middle East and structures its programs accordingly. That area is much too large, too diverse, too opaque, and too much in the grip of immoderate sectors to allow for much traction (as reflected in the experience of MEPI). It can absorb very large amounts of resources with little or no impact. Instead, the United States should pursue a new policy that is *asymmetric* and *selective.* As in the Cold War, U.S. efforts should avoid the opponent's center of gravity and instead concentrate on the partners, programs, and regions where U.S. support has the greatest likelihood of making an impact in the war of ideas.

With regard to partners, it will be important to identify the social sectors that would constitute the building blocks of the proposed networks. Priority should be given to groups and individuals that meet the criteria that we have identified for appropriate partners and that fall within these sectors:

1. Liberal and secular Muslim academics and intellectuals
2. Young moderate religious scholars
3. Community activists
4. Women's groups engaged in gender equality campaigns
5. Moderate journalists and writers.

The United States should ensure visibility and platforms for these individuals. For example, U.S. officials should ensure that individuals from these groups are included in congressional visits, making them better known to policymakers and helping to maintain U.S. support and resources for the public diplomacy effort.

Assistance programs should be organized around the sectors listed above, and would include

1. *Democratic education*, particularly programs that use Islamic texts and traditions for authoritative teachings that support democratic and pluralistic values.
2. *Media*. Support for moderate media is critical to combating media domination by anti-democratic and conservative Muslim elements.
3. *Gender equality*. The issue of women's rights is a major battleground in the war of ideas within Islam, and women's rights advocates operate in very adverse environments. Promotion of gender equality is a critical component of any project to empower moderate Muslims.
4. *Policy advocacy*. Islamists have political agendas, and moderates need to engage in policy advocacy as well. Advocacy activities are important in order to shape the political and legal environment in the Muslim world.

With regard to geographic focus, we propose a shift of priorities from the Middle East to the regions of the Muslim world where greater freedom of action is possible, the environment is more open to activism and influence, and success is more likely and more perceptible. The current approach focuses on the Middle East, recognizing that radical ideas originate in the Middle East and from there are disseminated to the rest of the Muslim world, including the Muslim diaspora communities in Europe and North America. An alternative approach is to seek to reverse the flow of ideas. Important texts originating from thinkers, intellectuals, activists, and leaders in the Muslim diaspora, in Turkey, in Indonesia, and elsewhere should be translated into Arabic and disseminated widely. This does not mean that core areas should be abandoned. Rather, the goal should be to hold the ground in expectation of opportunities for advancement, which can arise at any moment.

There is some "networking" of moderates currently going on, but it is random and insufficiently considered. Networking individuals and groups whose credentials as moderates have not been firmly established and networking pseudo-moderates not only are a waste of resources, but can be counterproductive. The Danish imams who caused the cartoon controversy to spiral into an international conflagration had earlier been presumed to be moderates and had been the beneficiaries of state support, including travel and networking opportunities. Closer scrutiny after the incident revealed that these individuals were not true moderates at all.

Public diplomacy currently lags behind the media curve and needs to pay closer attention to contemporary circumstances. Radio was an important medium during the Cold War, helping isolated populations gain better access to information. Today, citizens of the Muslim world are overwhelmed by a vast amount of often inaccurate and biased information, and content and delivery stand in a much more demanding relationship to each other. Radio Sawa and Al Hurra are perceived as proxies for the U.S. government and, despite their high cost, have not resulted in positively shaping attitudes toward the United States. We believe that the funds spent on Radio Sawa and Al Hurra television would be better spent supporting local media outlets and journalists that adhere to a democratic and pluralistic agenda.

Launching the Initiative

We propose to launch the initiative recommended in this report with a workshop, to be held in Washington or another appropriate venue, gathering a small, representative group of Muslim moderates. This workshop would serve to obtain their input and their support for the initiative and to prepare the agenda and list of participants for an international conference modeled on the Congress of Cultural Freedom.

If this event were successful, we would then work with the core group to hold an international conference in a venue of symbolic significance for Muslims, for instance, Córdoba in Spain, to launch a standing organization to combat Salafist extremism. The main components of this strategy are summarized below:

- Principal goals
  - Link Muslim liberals and moderates
  - Begin with a known and solid core group and build outward from there
  - Exceptions should only be made knowingly, selectively, and tactically
  - Reverse the flow of ideas (instead of Arab heartland > periphery, moderate periphery > Arab heartland)
  - Focus on areas of maximum obtainable success
  - Elsewhere, concentrate on holding ground and waiting for opportunities
- Some key implementation tools
  - Convene a small workshop of boots-on-the-ground liberals and moderates to help identify what they would need to become more effective
  - Tailor a set of pilot programs on the basis of these needs
  - Launch an international network of liberal and moderate Muslims, convening them in a location of symbolic salience
  - Reconfigure programs to concentrate on true moderates in locations that hold promise
  - Ensure visibility and platforms for them. For example, ensure that they are included in congressional visits and meetings with senior officials to make them better known to policymakers and to maintain support and resources for the effort.

APPENDIX A

U.S. Foreign Assistance Framework

Figure A.1
U.S. Foreign Assistance Framework as of October 12, 2006

Goal: "Helping to build and sustain democratic, well-governed states that will respond to the needs of their people and conduct themselves responsibly in the international system."

	Peace and Security	Governing Justly and Democratically	Investing in People	Economic Growth	Humanitarian Assistance	End Goal of US Foreign Assistance	Graduation Trajectory
Accounts within State/USAID	FMF, IMET, ESF, INCLE, NADR, PKO, ACI, SA-SEED	DA, SEED, FSA, DF, ESF, INCLE, IOAP, ACI	DA, TI, GSH, ESF, IDFA, IOAP, FSA, SEED, GHAI Title III	DA, TI, ESF, SEED, FSA, IOAP, Title II	IDFA, MRA, ERMA, Title II		
Other USG Agency Contributions							
Foreign Assistance Program Areas	➤ Counter-Terrorism ➤ Combating WMD ➤ Stabilization Operations and Defense Reform ➤ Counternarcotics ➤ Transnational Crime ➤ Conflict Mitigation and Response	➤ Rule of Law and Human Rights ➤ Good Governance ➤ Political Competition and Consensus-Building ➤ Civil Society	➤ Health ➤ Education ➤ Social Services and Protection for Vulnerable Populations	➤ Macroeconomic Foundation for Growth ➤ Trade and Investment ➤ Financial Sector ➤ Infrastructure ➤ Agriculture ➤ Private Sector Competitiveness ➤ Economic Opportunity ➤ Environment	➤ Protection, Assistance and Solutions ➤ Disaster Readiness ➤ Migration Management		

Category Definition

	Category Definition	Peace and Security	Governing Justly and Democratically	Investing in People	Economic Growth	Humanitarian Assistance	End Goal of US Foreign Assistance	Graduation Trajectory
Rebuilding Countries	States in or emerging from and rebuilding after internal or external conflict.	Prevent or mitigate state failure and/or violent conflict.	Assist in creating and/or stabilizing a legitimate and democratic government and a supportive environment for civil society and media.	Start or restart the delivery of critical social services, including health and educational facilities, and begin building or rebuilding institutional capacity.	Assist in the construction or reconstruction of key internal infrastructure and key market mechanisms to stabilize the economy.	Address immediate needs of refugees, displaced, and other affected groups.	Stable environment for good governance, increased availability of essential social services, and initial progress to create policies and institutions upon which future progress will rest.	Advance to the Developing or Transforming Category.
Developing Countries	States with low or lower-middle income, not yet meeting MCC performance criteria, and the criterion related to political rights.	Address key remaining challenges to security and law enforcement.	Support policies and programs that accelerate and strengthen public institutions and the creation of a more vibrant local government, civil society and media.	Encourage social policies that deepen the ability of institutions to establish appropriate roles for the public and private sector in service delivery.	Encourage economic policies and strengthen institutional capacity to promote broad-based growth.	Encourage reduced need for future HA by introducing prevention and mitigation strategies, while continuing to address emergency needs.	Continued progress in expanding and deepening democracy, strengthening public and private institutions, and supporting policies that promote economic growth and poverty reduction.	Advance to the Transforming Category.
Transforming Countries	States with low or lower-middle income, meeting MCC performance criteria, and the criterion related to political rights.	Nurture progress toward partnerships on security and law enforcement.	Provide limited resources and technical assistance to reinforce democratic institutions.	Provide financial resources and limited technical assistance to sustain improved livelihoods.	Provide financial resources and technical assistance to promote broad-based growth.	Address emergency needs on a short-term basis, as necessary.	Government, civil society and private sector institutions capable of sustaining development progress.	Advance to the Sustaining Partnership Category or graduate from foreign assistance.
Sustaining Partnership Countries	States with upper-middle income or greater for which U.S. support is provided to sustain partnerships, progress, and peace.	Support strategic partnerships addressing security, CT, WMD, and counter-narcotics.	Address issues of mutual interest.	Address issues of mutual interest.	Create and promote sustained partnerships on trade and investment.	Address emergency needs on a short-term basis, as necessary.	Continued partnership as strategically appropriate where U.S. support is necessary to maintain progress and peace.	Continue partnership or graduate from foreign assistance.
Restrictive Countries	States of concern where there are significant governance issues.	Prevent the acquisition/proliferation of WMD, support CT and counter-narcotics.	Foster effective democracy and responsible sovereignty. Create local capacity for fortification of civil society and path to democratic governance.	Address humanitarian needs.	Promote a market-based economy.	Address emergency needs on a short-term basis, as necessary.	Civil society empowered to demand more effective democracies and states respectful of human dignity, accountable to their citizens, and responsible towards their neighbors.	Advance to other relevant foreign assistance category.
Global or Regional	Activities that advance the five objectives, transcend a single country's borders, and are addressed outside a country strategy.						Achievement of foreign assistance goal and objectives.	Determined based on criteria specific to the global or regional objective.

SOURCE: U.S. Department of State. As of January 31, 2006:
http://www.state.gov/documents/organization/75118.pdf

Documents

The Ten Commandments of Democracy

From the platform of the Democratic Muslims[1]

1. We must all separate politics and religion, and we must never place religion above the laws of democracy.
2. We must all respect that all people have equal rights regardless of sex, ethnicity, sexual orientation or religious beliefs.
3. No person must ever incite to hatred, and we must never allow hatred to enter our hearts.
4. No person must ever use or encourage violence—no matter how frustrated or wronged we feel, or how just our cause.
5. We must all make use of dialogue—always.
6. We must all show respect for the freedom of expression, also of those with whom we disagree the most.
7. No person can claim or assign to others a place apart, neither as superior persons, as inferior persons or as eternal victims.
8. We must all treat other people's national and religious symbols as we wish them to treat ours—flag burning and graffiti on churches, mosques and synagogues are insults that hinder dialogue and increase the repression of the other party.
9. We must all mind our manners in public. Public space is not a stage on which to vent one's aggressions or to spread fear and

---

[1] Originally voiced by Naser Khader in 2002. Reproduced from Khader's Web page.

hate, but should be a forum for visions and arguments, where the best must win support.

10. We must all stand up for our opponent if he or she is subjected to spiteful treatment.

Right Islam vs. Wrong Islam

Abdurrahman Wahid[2]

News organizations report that Osama bin Laden has obtained a religious edict from a misguided Saudi cleric, justifying the use of nuclear weapons against America and the infliction of mass casualties. It requires great emotional strength to confront the potential ramifications of this fact. Yet can anyone doubt that those who joyfully incinerate the occupants of office buildings, commuter trains, hotels and nightclubs would leap at the chance to magnify their damage a thousandfold?

Imagine the impact of a single nuclear bomb detonated in New York, London, Paris, Sydney or L.A.! What about two or three? The entire edifice of modern civilization is built on economic and technological foundations that terrorists hope to collapse with nuclear attacks like so many fishing huts in the wake of a tsunami.

Just two small, well-placed bombs devastated Bali's tourist economy in 2002 and sent much of its population back to the rice fields and out to sea, to fill their empty bellies. What would be the effect of a global economic crisis in the wake of attacks far more devastating than those of Bali or 9/11?

It is time for people of good will from every faith and nation to recognize that a terrible danger threatens humanity. We cannot afford to continue "business as usual" in the face of this existential threat. Rather, we must set aside our international and partisan bickering, and join to confront the danger that lies before us.

An extreme and perverse ideology in the minds of fanatics is what directly threatens us (specifically, Wahhabi/Salafi ideology—a minority fundamentalist religious cult fueled by petrodollars). Yet underlying, enabling and exacerbating this threat of religious extremism is a global crisis of misunderstanding.

---

[2] Kyai Haji Abdurrahman Wahid is a former president of Indonesia and senior advisor to the Libforall Foundation. This piece appeared in *The Wall Street Journal* on December 30, 2005.

All too many Muslims fail to grasp Islam, which teaches one to be lenient towards others and to understand their value systems, knowing that these are tolerated by Islam as a religion. The essence of Islam is encapsulated in the words of the Quran, "For you, your religion; for me, my religion." That is the essence of tolerance. Religious fanatics—either purposely or out of ignorance—pervert Islam into a dogma of intolerance, hatred and bloodshed. They justify their brutality with slogans such as "Islam is above everything else." They seek to intimidate and subdue anyone who does not share their extremist views, regardless of nationality or religion. While a few are quick to shed blood themselves, countless millions of others sympathize with their violent actions, or join in the complicity of silence.

This crisis of misunderstanding—of Islam by Muslims themselves—is compounded by the failure of governments, people of other faiths, and the majority of well-intentioned Muslims to resist, isolate and discredit this dangerous ideology. The crisis thus afflicts Muslims and non-Muslims alike, with tragic consequences. Failure to understand the true nature of Islam permits the continued radicalization of Muslims world-wide, while blinding the rest of humanity to a solution which hides in plain sight.

The most effective way to overcome Islamist extremism is to explain what Islam truly is to Muslims and non-Muslims alike. Without that explanation, people will tend to accept the unrefuted extremist view—further radicalizing Muslims, and turning the rest of the world against Islam itself.

Accomplishing this task will be neither quick nor easy. In recent decades, Wahhabi/Salafi ideology has made substantial inroads throughout the Muslim world. Islamic fundamentalism has become a well-financed, multifaceted global movement that operates like a juggernaut in much of the developing world, and even among immigrant Muslim communities in the West. To neutralize the virulent ideology that underlies fundamentalist terrorism and threatens the very foundations of modern civilization, we must identify its advocates, understand their goals and strategies, evaluate their strengths and weaknesses, and effectively counter their every move. What we are talking about is nothing less than a global struggle for the soul of Islam.

The Sunni (as opposed to Shiite) fundamentalists' goals generally include: claiming to restore the perfection of the early Islam practiced by Muhammad and his companions, who are known in Arabic as *al-Salaf al-Salih*, "the Righteous Ancestors"; establishing a utopian society based on these Salafi principles, by imposing their interpretation of Islamic law on all members of society; annihilating local variants of Islam in the name of authenticity and purity; transforming Islam from a personal faith into an authoritarian political system; establishing a pan-Islamic caliphate governed according to the strict tenets of Salafi Islam, and often conceived as stretching from Morocco to Indonesia and the Philippines; and, ultimately, bringing the entire world under the sway of their extremist ideology.

Fundamentalist strategy is often simple as well as brilliant. Extremists are quick to drape themselves in the mantle of Islam and declare their opponents *kafir*, or infidels, and thus smooth the way for slaughtering nonfundamentalist Muslims. Their theology rests upon a simplistic, literal and highly selective reading of the Quran and Sunnah (prophetic traditions), through which they seek to entrap the world-wide Muslim community in the confines of their narrow ideological grasp. Expansionist by nature, most fundamentalist groups constantly probe for weakness and an opportunity to strike, at any time or place, to further their authoritarian goals.

The armed *ghazis* (Islamic warriors) raiding from New York to Jakarta, Istanbul, Baghdad, London and Madrid are only the tip of the iceberg, forerunners of a vast and growing population that shares their radical views and ultimate objectives. The formidable strengths of this worldwide fundamentalist movement include:

1) An aggressive program with clear ideological and political goals; 2) immense funding from oil-rich Wahhabi sponsors; 3) the ability to distribute funds in impoverished areas to buy loyalty and power; 4) a claim to and aura of religious authenticity and Arab prestige; 5) an appeal to Islamic identity, pride and history; 6) an ability to blend into the much larger traditionalist masses and blur the distinction between moderate Islam and their brand of religious extremism; 7) full-time commitment by its agents/leadership; 8) networks of Islamic schools that propagate extremism; 9) the absence of organized opposition in

the Islamic world; 10) a global network of fundamentalist imams who guide their flocks to extremism; 11) a well-oiled "machine" established to translate, publish and distribute Wahhabi/Salafi propaganda and disseminate its ideology throughout the world; 12) scholarships for locals to study in Saudi Arabia and return with degrees and indoctrination, to serve as future leaders; 13) the ability to cross national and cultural borders in the name of religion; 14) Internet communication; and 15) the reluctance of many national governments to supervise or control this entire process.

We must employ effective strategies to counter each of these fundamentalist strengths. This can be accomplished only by bringing the combined weight of the vast majority of peace-loving Muslims, and the non-Muslim world, to bear in a coordinated global campaign whose goal is to resolve the crisis of misunderstanding that threatens to engulf our entire world.

An effective counterstrategy must be based upon a realistic assessment of our own strengths and weaknesses in the face of religious extremism and terror. Disunity, of course, has proved fatal to countless human societies faced with a similar existential threat. A lack of seriousness in confronting the imminent danger is likewise often fatal. Those who seek to promote a peaceful and tolerant understanding of Islam must overcome the paralyzing effects of inertia, and harness a number of actual or potential strengths, which can play a key role in neutralizing fundamentalist ideology. These strengths not only are assets in the struggle with religious extremism, but in their mirror form they point to the weakness at the heart of fundamentalist ideology. They are: 1) Human dignity, which demands freedom of conscience and rejects the forced imposition of religious views; 2) the ability to mobilize immense resources to bring to bear on this problem, once it is identified and a global commitment is made to solve it; 3) the ability to leverage resources by supporting individuals and organizations that truly embrace a peaceful and tolerant Islam; 4) nearly 1,400 years of Islamic traditions and spirituality, which are inimical to fundamentalist ideology; 5) appeals to local and national—as well as Islamic—culture/traditions/pride; 6) the power of the feminine spirit, and the fact that half of humanity consists of women, who have an inherent stake in the outcome of this struggle; 7) traditional and Sufi leadership and masses, who are not yet radicalized (strong numeric advantage: 85% to 90% of the world's 1.3 billion Muslims); 8) the ability to harness networks of Islamic schools to propagate a peaceful and tolerant Islam; 9) the natural tendency of like-minded people to work together when alerted to a common danger; 10) the ability to form a global network of like-minded individuals, organizations and opinion leaders to promote moderate and progressive ideas throughout the Muslim world; 11) the existence of a counterideology, in the form of traditional, Sufi and modern Islamic teachings, and the ability to translate such works into key languages; 12) the benefits of modernity, for all its flaws, and the widespread appeal of popular culture; 13) the ability to cross national and cultural borders in the name of religion; 14) Internet communications, to disseminate progressive views—linking and inspiring like-minded individuals and organizations throughout the world; 15) the nation-state; and 16) the universal human desire for freedom, justice and a better life for oneself and loved ones.

Though potentially decisive, most of these advantages remain latent or diffuse, and require mobilization to be effective in confronting fundamentalist ideology. In addition, no effort to defeat religious extremism can succeed without ultimately cutting off the flow of petrodollars used to finance that extremism, from Leeds to Jakarta.

Only by recognizing the problem, putting an end to the bickering within and between nation-states, and adopting a coherent long-term plan (executed with international leadership and commitment) can we begin to apply the brakes to the rampant spread of extremist ideas and hope to resolve the world's crisis of misunderstanding before the global economy and modern civilization itself begin to crumble in the face of truly devastating attacks.

Muslims themselves can and must propagate an understanding of the "right" Islam, and thereby discredit extremist ideology. Yet to accomplish this task requires the understanding and support of like-minded individuals, organizations and governments throughout the world. Our goal must be to illuminate the hearts and minds of humanity, and offer a compelling alternate vision of Islam, one that banishes the fanatical ideology of hatred to the darkness from which it emerged.

Text of the Fatwa Declared Against Osama Bin Laden by the Islamic Commission of Spain[3]

Doctrinal foundation

In the Koran, The Book revealed to Humanity as a guide, God orders Muslims to acquire an excellence in ethical and moral behavior. Islamic morality rests on values such as peace, tolerance, mercy or compassion.

The Koran reminds Muslims they are responsible before God for their behavior and treatment of all peoples; whether they are also Muslim or not.

In this sense, Muslims are forced to seek out good for themselves, their families, their neighbors and society in general.

"Do good unto others as God has done unto you; and do not wish to plant the seeds of corruption upon Earth, for God does not love those who sow corruption". (28:77).

The term "corruption" includes here all forms of anarchy and terrorism that undermine or destroy peace and Muslim security.

Muslims, therefore, are not only forbidden from committing crimes against innocent people, but are responsible before God to stop those people who have the intention to do so, since these people "are planting the seeds of corruption on Earth".

In reference to the treatment towards non-Muslims, the *aleya* herself says in 60:8:

"As long as they do not fight you because of your religion nor expel you from your homes, you are not prohibited to treat them with the greatest deference (birr) or justice, since, God loves the righteous".

The concept of "birr" in this *aleya* makes reference to the way in which somebody must treat parents and relatives. The Prophet explains further in the two main collections of *hadices* (Bujari and Muslim):

"By God, those are not true believers who are feared by their neighbors for their malice".

The Prophet even encouraged believers to be kind to animals and prohibited them from doing damage to or burden animals with work.

---

3   The original Spanish-language text can be found on WebIslam.

A *hadiz* tells us of the time The Prophet said to a man who gave to drink a thirsty dog that he was pardoned of all his sins by this single action.

It was asked to him then:

"Oh Messenger of God, then will we be compensated by our kindness towards all animals?" The Prophet answered: "There is a reward for kindness towards any animal or human being". (Sahih Muslim, 2244, and Sahih Al-Bujari, 2466).

The Koran does not encourage Muslims to return evil deeds with evil deeds; on the contrary, it calls believers to respond to evil deeds with good actions.

"But (as) good and evil cannot be compared, counter evil with something better. Henceforth, he whosoever existed in enmity with you, shall become a true friend". (41:34).

God also indicates in the Koran that the Garden (Paradise) has been prepared for those who work on His Cause, in days of prosperity and in days of deprivation; as well as for those who keep in check their wrath and pardon their neighbors, because God loves those who do good (3:135).

"For those who persevere in doing good, the supreme good awaits them. Their faces will not be overshadowed by darkness or humiliation (in the Day of the Judgment). They are destined to Paradise, where they will reside (eternally)". (10:26).

"Remember that any attempt to make up for evil can become evil. Therefore, those who forgive their enemies and make peace with them, will receive his reward from God, because certainly God does not love malefactors". (42:40).

The hatred of God towards murder is manifested in the *aleyas* that speak of Abel in the Surah of the Served Table:

"and Cain said: "Be certain that I will kill you" (5:27). To which Abel responded:

"Even if you raised your hand to kill me, I will not raise my hand to kill you: in truth, I fear God, the Provider of all worlds."

After the murder of Abel, God says:

"We declare to the children of Israel that those who kill a human being—not being to punish murder or the plating of corruption on

Earth—will be treated as if they had killed all of humanity; and whosoever saves a life, will be treated as if they had saved the life of all of humanity."

Let it be noted that the reference to the children of Israel does not diminish the universal validity of its message.

The Prophet also reminded us that murder was the second of the greatest sins (Sahih Al-Bujari: 6871, and Sahih Muslim: 88) that can be committed, and noticed that on Judgment Day, the first cases to be judged will be those dealing with bloodshed (Sahih Muslim: 1678, and Sahih Al-Bujari: 6533).

The own concept of war established in the Koran has an exclusively defensive tone:

"and you fight for the cause of God against those who fight you, but you do not commit aggressions, since certainly, God does not love the aggressors" (2:190).

As Muhammad Asad in his *tafsir* (interpretation of the Koran) says: "Most commentators agree that the expression *taatadu* means, in this context, "you do not commit aggression." The defensive character of combat "for the cause of God"—that is to say, because of the ethical principles ordered by God, is evident by the reference to "those who fight you". . . and it is clarified furthermore in the *aleya* 22:39: "It is allowed (to fight) those who have injured them unjustly"; that it is, according to all our traditions our first (and therefore fundamental) Koranic reference to the question of *yihad*.

Within the context of defensive warfare, The Prophet imposed strict limits destined to safeguard lives and properties. Thus, the Prophet Muhammad prohibited to kill, in the case of warlike conflict, women, children and civilians (Sahih Muslim: 1744, and Sahih Al-Bujari: 3015).

He also said whosoever killed anyone who had signed a treaty or agreement with Muslims, would not smell the fragrance of Paradise (Sahih Al-Bujari: 3166, and Ibn Mayah: 2686).

In light of these and other Islamic texts, the terrorist acts of Osama ben Laden and his organization Al Qaida—who look to fill with fear the hearts of defenseless people; who engage in the destruction of buildings or properties thus involving the death of civilians, like women, children, and other beings—are strictly prohibited and are the object of a full condemnation from Islam.

Therefore, the perpetration of terrorist acts under the pretext "of defending the oppressed nations of the world or the rights of Muslims" does not have any justification in Islam.

There is no doubt Muslims have the legitimate right to react against any aggression or any situation of oppression. Nevertheless, such reaction should not give rise to blind or irrational hatred:

"you do not let your hatred towards those who prevent you access to the House of Inviolable Adoration (that is to say, to the fulfillment of your religious obligations) take you to transgression (the limits); but on the contrary, [it should encourage you to] collaborate in fomenting virtue and acknowledgment of God and not to collaborate in fomenting evil and enmity". (5:2).

Likewise, the Koran indicates, in reference to those who hypocritically claim to follow the Bible, that whenever anyone lights the fire of war, God extinguishes it (5:64). God also condemns those nations that violate international treaties and initiate wars (8:56) and requests that everything is done to defeat them (8:60), but if they are inclined to peace, then Muslims will have to follow suit as well (8:61).

Given all of this, it is necessary to point out that terrorism and extremism contradict human nature and the lessons of Islam.

Muslims must know that terrorism is a threat against Islam and that it is damaging to our religion and to Muslims. A correct Islamic formation in *madrasas* and Islamic universities will allow everybody to understand that Islam is a religion of peace and that it repudiates all acts of terrorism and indiscriminate death.

The presence of signs like arrogance, fanaticism, extremism or religious intolerance in an individual or group, let's us know they have broken with Islam and the traditions of the Prophet Muhammad.

The perpetration of terrorist acts supposes a rupture of such magnitude with Islamic teaching that it allows to affirm that the individuals or groups who have perpetrated them have stopped being Muslim and have put themselves outside the sphere of Islam. Such groups distort and manipulate basic Islamic concepts, like the one of *yihad*, by imposing upon them their particular interpretation and criteria.

In fact, groups that use names and languages relative to Islam, discredit with their actions the image of Islam and serve the interests of their enemies. Their actions incite Islamophobia in countries in which Muslims are a minority, and destroy the relationships of cooperation and neighborliness between Muslims and non-Muslim. Their actions provide a false image of Islam, which is precisely what the enemies of Islam strive to offer to the world.

These extremist groups bring indiscriminate death, even to other Muslims. We must remember here that The Prophet showed that Muslims who kill other Muslims turn *kafir* (unbelieving).

In this same sense, if a Muslim or a group of them commit a terrorist act, this individual or group would be breaking the laws of Islam and leaving the guide of God and the way of the *Din*.

"God does not grant his guidance to people who deliberately do evil". (9:109).

Heretofore we declare in good faith the following resolution:

1. That Islam rejects terrorism in all its manifestations, being the death or damage to innocent human beings or to their properties.
2. That Islam is the main victim of terrorist attacks made by some groups that falsely call themselves "Islamic", inasmuch as such attacks not only take the life of numerous Muslims, but because they also damage the image of Islam by fomenting feelings of Islamophobia and serving the interests of the enemies of Islam.
3. That these groups try to conceal their deviation through falsehoods and manipulated interpretations of sacred texts, in an attempt to gain support among Muslims or to recruit new followers. This fraud must be denounced with force by the wise people and leaders of Islam worldwide.
4. That those who commit terrorist acts violate Koranic teachings and thus turn apostates who have left Islam.
5. That the duty of every Muslim is to fight actively against terrorism, in accordance with the Koranic mandate that estab-

lishes the obligation to prevent corruption from overtaking the Earth.

Based on what has been exposed, it comes to dictate:
That according to the Sharia, all who declare *halal* or allowed what God has declared *haram* or prohibited, like the killing of innocent people in terrorist attacks, have become *Kafir Murtadd Mustahlil*, that's to say an apostate, by trying to make a crime such as the murder of innocents, *halal* (istihlal); a crime forbidden by the Sacred Koran and the Sunna of the Prophet Muhammad, God bless him and save him.

As long as Osama ben Laden and his organization defend the legality of terrorism and try to base it on the Sacred Koran and the Sunna, they are committing the crime of *istihlal* and they have become ipso facto apostates (*kafir murtadd*), who should not be considered Muslim nor be treated as such.

To which we declare that Osama ben Laden and his organization Al Qaida, responsible for the horrible crimes against the innocents who vilely were assassinated in the terrorist attack of 11 March in Madrid, are outside the parameters of Islam; and the same goes to all who wield the Sacred Koran and The Prophet's Sunna to commit terrorist acts.

To which we declare that the alleged political reasonings by Osama ben Laden and his organization regarding the recovery of *Al Andalus*; having been made public and become well-known by all, completely contradict the divine will that has been expressed clearly through history; being that God is the Lord of History and everything that happens, has happened or will happen; that he is Divine Aim and Favor and must be considered as such in any event by Muslims, for whom God is Giver of Goods; and that not even the best of conspirators are creatures with the capacity to judge or question what the Divine Will has decreed.

The tragedy of *Al Andalus*, the genocide of Muslims and their expulsion from Spain, the natural mother country of all of them, is to be judged by God alone; and to the servant, to accept the Divine Decree and be thankful.

In reference to the breach of the Capitulations of Santa Fe signed by the Catholic King and Queen and the King of the Islamic Kingdom of Granada, we declare that with the signing of the Agreements of Cooperation of 1992—between the Spanish State and the legal representatives of the Spanish Muslims known as The Islamic Commission of Spain—it is taken as conclusive all vindication of legal or political type, whereas the Agreement recognizes in its introduction that "Islam is part of the identity of Spain." This recognition, along with what is stipulated in the Agreement, settles definitively the issue from a legal or political point of view.

The Agreement of Cooperation of 1992 is the new frame we have given ourselves to bring together the Spanish State and Spanish Muslims. The Agreement represents the explicit will of Spanish Muslims; and nobody outside of this community, whether they are called Ben Laden or Al Qaida or by any other name, has the right to meddle with the matters of our Islamic community.

Based on this fatwa, we have requested the national government and Spanish mass media to stop using the words *Islam* or *Islamic* to describe these malefactors, given they are not Muslim nor have any relationship with our Umma or Islamic Community; instead needing to call them Al Qaida terrorists, but without using Islamic as an adjective, since as it has been declared above, they are not legally so.

Likewise, we ask those in charge of mass media to acknowledge what has been stated here and to proceed from now on under the criteria exposed above; particularly, by not tying Islam nor Muslims with any terrorist acts; especially if the acts appear dressed with any Islamic language or pretension.

Mansur Escudero Bedate
Secretary General of The Islamic Commission of Spain
In Cordova, 11 March 2005

Manifesto: Together Facing the New Totalitarianism[4]

After having overcome fascism, Nazism, and Stalinism, the world now faces a new totalitarian global threat: Islamism.

We, writers, journalists, intellectuals, call for resistance to religious totalitarianism and for the promotion of freedom, equal opportunity and secular values for all.

The recent events, which occurred after the publication of drawings of Muhammed in European newspapers, have revealed the necessity of the struggle for these universal values. This struggle will not be won by arms, but in the ideological field. It is not a clash of civilizations nor an antagonism of West and East that we are witnessing, but a global struggle that confronts democrats and theocrats.

Like all totalitarianisms, Islamism is nurtured by fears and frustrations. The hate preachers bet on these feelings in order to form battalions destined to impose a liberticidal and unegalitarian world. But we clearly and firmly state: nothing, not even despair, justifies the choice of obscurantism, totalitarianism and hatred. Islamism is a reactionary ideology, which kills equality, freedom and secularism wherever it is present. Its success can only lead to a world of domination: man's domination of woman, the Islamists' domination of all the others. To counter this, we must assure universal rights to oppressed or discriminated people.

We reject "cultural relativism", which consists in accepting that men and women of Muslim culture should be deprived of the right to equality, freedom and secular values in the name of respect for cultures and traditions. We refuse to renounce our critical spirit out of fear of being accused of "Islamophobia", an unfortunate concept which confuses criticism of Islam as a religion with stigmatisation of its believers.

We plead for the universality of freedom of expression, so that a critical spirit may be exercised on all continents, against all abuses and all dogmas.

---

[4] First published in *Morgenavisen Jyllands Posten,* February 28, 2006.

We appeal to democrats and free spirits of all countries that our century should be one of Enlightenment, not of obscurantism.

Ayaan Hirsi Ali
Chahla Chafiq
Caroline Fourest
Bernard-Henri Lévy
Irshad Manji
Mehdi Mozaffari
Maryam Namazie
Taslima Nasreen
Salman Rushdie
Antoine Sfeir
Philippe Val
Ibn Warraq

Stop Capitulating to Threats—A Manifesto[5]

Preserving freedom of expression is the cheapest and most sustainable way to govern a country and keep it stable. This was the unsolicited advice of Akbar Gandji to the Iranian spiritual leader Ayatollah Khamenei. The Iranian journalist and political philosopher Gandji was jailed over six years ago. For how long, would be the obvious question in a state subject to the rule of law, where the government acts in accordance with previously published statutes. But the possible date of Gandji's release is as arbitrary as were his prosecution and sentencing. The tragic story of freedom of expression as a human right has a special place in the worldwide picture of the infringement of human rights. The reason is obvious: suppression of freedom of expression is often a prelude to other human rights abuses.

In most Islamic countries and cultures freedom of expression is unknown. And that is nothing new. Chauvinism, ethnic nationalism and religious fanaticism often generate an aggressive attitude to dissidents.

Recently, like other countries, the Netherlands has been confronted with these phenomena. It may not yet have impinged on everyone, but it is true. Before I deal with it more fully, I would first like to discuss a manifestation of it in the Islamic world: the murder of the intellectual Kasrawi.

Whenever intellectuals in an Islamic country wish to engage in critical debates, they will face serious problems. A notorious example is what happened to Ahmad Kasrawi (1891–1946). This jurist, historian and journalist is unknown in the Western world, but had a great reputation in Iran as a champion of human rights and liberal constitutional principles. Kasrawi had also researched the political theology of Islam, and in his work had criticised the Shiite concept of the imam. A number of ayatollahs accused him of kuffer (disbelief), and his books were publicly burnt. While the Allied troops in Iran (the Americans

---

[5]   Professor Afshin Ellian is Professor of Social Cohesion, Citizenship and Multicultural Studies, Leiden University Faculty of Law. This manifesto was read by Afshin at an international literature festival in Winternachten in The Hague on January 20, 2006, and subsequently published on his personal blog.

based in Teheran), excitedly watched the collapse of Nazism in Europe, a strange event took place in Teheran. A talib (the singular form of taliban = religious pupil) called Nawab Safawie had set up a secret organisation to fight "the enemies of Islam" by force, the Islamic Fedayin. Safawie went to an ayatollah and asked for a fatwa against Kasrawi. His request was granted, that is, a fatwa requiring the death penalty. On 28 April 1945 Safawie carried out an assassination attempt on Kasrawi in broad daylight. Kasrawi survived the attack. The culprit was arrested, but subsequently managed to escape to Najaf (Iraq), where he headed a terrorist group for a while.

March 1946. The continent of Europe was free once more. But in Teheran the struggle over freedom of expression erupted again. On the basis of charges by a number of Taliban, Kasrawi was summonsed to appear before the public prosecutor in Teheran on a charge of sacrilegious blasphemy. Initially the Iranian legal system was reluctant to prosecute him. At first they hoped to be able to refer the case to the Allied forces, appealing to the Allied treaty guaranteeing freedom of expression to all Iranians. However, the Allies considered the case an internal matter. It has since emerged that the Americans persuaded the Iranian police to guard Kasrawi's house. The High Court, Teheran, 11 March 1946, the day on which Kasrawi was to be tried. Through the press eight members of the Fedayin of Islam knew the time and place of the hearing. They stormed the court, killing Kasrawi and his secretary. The perpetrators used both firearms to kill the writer and a knife to mutilate his body.

The parallel with the Netherlands may be gradually becoming clear. Because this dangerous tradition has unfortunately been exported to Europe. On 2 November 2004 the film-maker and columnist Theo van Gogh was murdered. Europeans were deeply shocked by his assassination. The culprit, Mohammed Bouyeri stated in court that he had acted from religious conviction. Mohammed Bouyeri's concluding, almost magical words were bewildering, for the average Dutch citizen at least:

'Another thing about your criticism. Perhaps by Moroccans you mean Muslims. I don't blame you, because the same law that calls on me to behead all those who denigrate Allah and his Prophet, that same law calls on me not to settle in this country. Or at least not in a country where freedom of speech, as described by the public prosecutor, is proclaimed. (…) And I think that those police officers who were confronted with me on 2 November, have the right to know: I did not shoot to spare you, I shot to kill and to be killed.'

In 1989 the Berlin Wall fell. It was a symbol of the totalitarian Marxism that had held the Eastern-bloc states and part of Western Europe in its grip for almost a century. In the Soviet Union and its satellite states countless writers were subjugated and had their freedom restricted. But that same year a new form of totalitarianism reared its head: the fatwa against Salman Rushdie issued by Ayatollah Khomeiny which—very much in the tradition of the murder of Kasrawi—also called for the murder of a writer, this time a British one. The attack on Rushdie's Satanic Verses could perhaps be seen as the as the birth of Talibanism in Europe: book burnings, threats and terrorist attacks on the publishers and translators ensued. The European states and their intelligentsia refused to give in to these terrorist threats. The International Writers' Parliament also had the courage to resist supra-national forms of terror. But Europe seems to have lost that resilience. Unfortunately after the murder of Van Gogh there was a change of heart on freedom of expression. This concerns film Submission, made by Theo van Gogh and the Dutch member of parliament Ayaan Hrisi Ali about the oppression of women in Islamic culture.

The film Submission has not been shown since 2 November 2004.

In fact, the film is under an informal screening ban. This ban has been decreed not by any authority but by criminal groups threatening terrorist acts. In 2005 in the Netherlands the producers do not dare show a ten-minute film to the public because the safety of their production company cannot be guaranteed. We are beginning to regard this as normal in the Netherlands as elsewhere. Actually, why are we fighting for freedom of expression for artists and journalists in autocratic countries like Iran when the situation in the Netherlands is starting to look suspiciously similar?

Fortunately the Satanic Verses are being republished here, but is that really still feasible? Hasn't the book become like a lighted cigarette in a powder keg? Free speech is in danger of being increasingly restricted by invoking "Islamophobia" and "racism." And some intellectuals have already capitulated. For example, the opera Aisha was called off in Rotterdam in 2001, because the wife of the Prophet was depicted on stage. The production had to be cancelled because a number of actresses felt threatened. Recently a columnist on the national daily NRC Handelsblad, Hasna el Maroudi was forced to abandon her column because of threats of violence from the Moroccan community. What has happened to civil courage? Why do we hear nothing from the publishers, artists, media and colleagues of people who have capitulated about the consequences of this voluntary capitulation?

We should expect civil courage not only from those who are threatened, but also from those around them, their publishers, producers, colleagues, etc.

I have encountered political-religious intolerance before. I know how it begins, how it develops. Let no one say that we are in the grip of Islamophobia or racism. Believe me—they are very different. Luther was not a Catholicophobe. He was critical of the church. Voltaire was not a religiophobe. He was simply critical of the intolerant manifestations of religion. Should the Reformation have been warded off on the grounds that Luther "must not stigmatise all Catholics"?

Intellectuals themselves are increasingly calling for self-censorship and politically correct reporting of intolerant tendencies. Has this country lost its appetite for freedom? Has the country where Pierre Bayle and John Locke published their books become a land of veiled opinions?

No one is trying stigmatise or lump together all the adherents of a particular faith. To repeat that constantly that is a malicious allegation. But what must be maintained is the opportunity to criticise religion freely, even if that upsets the radicals.

In the Netherlands of all places we have tradition to uphold. We would have found it unacceptable in bookshops had refused to sell the Satanic Verses. This matter is no longer a local affair. We must overcome our fears through a form of international solidarity. Now it is the Netherlands that needs such solidarity. Therefore I believe that the matter should be internationalised.

An international committee must be set up to administer the film Submission and make it available to everyone (who wishes to show it). In this way the ban on showings can be circumvented. A democratic culture cannot function without civil courage. So let us show courage and lift the ban on the film Submission.

References

Books

Aboul-Enein, Youssef, and Sherifa Zuhur, *Islamic Rulings on Warfare*, Carlisle, Pa.: Strategic Studies Institute, U.S. Army War College, October 2004. As of December 11, 2006:
www.strategicstudiesinstitute.army.mil/pdffiles/PUB588.pdf

Bar, Shmuel, *Warrant for Terror: The Fatwas of Radical Islam and the Duty of Jihad*, Lanham, Md.: Rowan & Littlefield Publishers, 2006.

Benard, Cheryl, *Civil Democratic Islam*, Santa Monica, Calif.: RAND Corporation, MR-1716-CMEPP, 2003. As of December 11, 2006:
http://www.rand.org/pubs/monograph_reports/MR1716/

———, *Freedom Bytes: The Internet and the War of Ideas*, Santa Monica, Calif.: RAND Corporation, WR-370-SR, forthcoming.

Bencheikh, Soheib, *Marianne et le Prophete, L'Islam dans la France Laique*, Paris: Bernard Grasset Publishers, 1998.

Carew, Anthony, *Labour Under the Marshall Plan: The Politics of Productivity and the Marketing of Management Science*, Detroit, Mich.: Wayne State University Press, 1987.

Carothers, Thomas, and Marina S. Ottaway, *Uncharted Journey: Promoting Democracy in the Middle East*, Washington, D.C.: Carnegie Endowment for International Peace, 2005.

Carothers, Thomas, Marina S. Ottaway, Amy Hawthorne, and Daniel Brumberg, *Democratic Mirage in the Middle East*, Carnegie Policy Brief No. 20, Washington, D.C.: Carnegie Endowment for International Peace, October 2002.

Charfi, Mohammed, *Islam and Liberty: The Historical Misunderstanding*, trans. Patrick Camiller, New York: Zed Books, 2005.

Cole, Juan, *Sacred Space and Holy War: The Politics, Culture and History of Shi'ite Islam*, London: I.B. Tauris, 2002.

Coleman, Peter, *The Liberal Conspiracy: The Congress for Cultural Freedom and the Struggle for the Mind of Postwar Europe*, New York: Free Press, 1989.

Garfinkle, Adam, ed., *A Practical Guide to Winning the War on Terrorism*, Stanford, Calif.: Hoover Institution Press, 2004.

Grose, Peter, *Operation Rollback: America's Secret War Behind the Iron Curtain*, Boston: Houghton Mifflin, 2000.

Habeck, Mary, *Knowing the Enemy: Jihadist Ideology and the War on Terror*, New Haven, Conn.: Yale University Press, 2006.

Hefner, Robert W., *Civil Islam: Muslims and Democratization in Indonesia*, Princeton, N.J.: Princeton University Press, 2000.

Hixson, Walter L., *George F. Kennan: Cold War Iconoclast*, New York: Columbia University Press, 1989.

Hobson, John, *The Eastern Origins of Western Civilization*, Cambridge: Cambridge University Press, 2004.

Hunter, Shireen, ed., *Islam, Europe's Second Religion: The New Social, Cultural, and Political Landscape*, Westport, Conn.: Praeger, 2002.

Kennan, George, *Memoirs: 1925–1950*, Boston: Little, Brown, 1967.

Kepel, Gilles, *Jihad: The Trail of Political Islam*, Cambridge, Mass.: Belknap Press, 2002.

Khader, Naser, *Khader.dk: Sammenførte Erindringer*, [Copenhagen]: Aschehoug, 2000.

Kurzman, Charles, ed., *Liberal Islam: A Sourcebook*, New York: Oxford University Press, 1998.

Lewis, Bernard, *The Crisis of Islam*, New York: The Modern Library, 2003.

Lucas, Scott, *Freedom's War: The American Crusade Against the Soviet Union*, New York: New York University Press, 1999.

Maarif, Ahmad Syafii, *Mencari Autenisitas Dalam Kegalauan*, Jakarta: PSAP, 2004.

McCullough, David, *Truman*, New York: Simon and Schuster, 1992.

Meuleman, Johan, ed., *Islam in the Era of Globalization*, Jakarta: Indonesian-Netherlands Cooperation in Islamic Studies, 2001.

Meyer, Cord, *Facing Reality: From World Federalism to the CIA*, New York: Harper & Row, 1980.

Miscamble, Wilson, *George F. Kennan and the Making of American Foreign Policy 1947–1950*, Princeton, N.J.: Princeton University Press, 1992.

Mitrovich, Gregory, *Undermining the Kremlin: America's Strategy to Subvert the Soviet Block, 1947–1956*, Ithaca, N.Y.: Cornell University Press, 2000.

Mozaffari, Mehdi, *Fatwa: Violence and Discourtesy*, Aarhus, Denmark: Aarhus University Press, July 1998.

Muzaffar, Chandra, *Islamic Resurgence in Malaysia,* Kuala Lumpur: Penerbit Fajar Bakti Sdn. Bhd., 1987.

Puddington, Arch, *Broadcasting Freedom: The Cold War Triumph of Radio Free Europe and Radio Liberty,* Lexington, Ky.: University Press of Kentucky, 2000.

Rabasa, Angel, *Political Islam in Southeast Asia: Moderates, Radicals and Terrorists*, International Institute for Strategic Studies Adelphi Paper No. 358, Oxford: Oxford University Press, 2003.

Rabasa, Angel M., Cheryl Benard, Peter Chalk, C. Christine Fair, Theodore Karasik, Rollie Lal, Ian Lesser, and David Thaler, *The Muslim World After 9/11*, Santa Monica, Calif.: RAND Corporation, MG-246-AF, 2004. As of December 11, 2006:
http://www.rand.org/pubs/monographs/MG246/

Roy, Oliver, *Globalized Islam: The Search for a New Ummah,* New York: Columbia University Press, 2004.

Sajoo, Amyn B., ed., *Civil Society in the Muslim World: Contemporary Perspectives,* London: I.B. Tauris Publishers, 2002.

Satloff, Robert, *The Battle of Ideas in the War on Terror,* Washington, D.C.: Washington Institute for Near East Policy, 2004.

Schwartz, Stephen, *The Two Faces of Islam: The House of Saud from Tradition to Terror,* New York: Doubleday, 2002.

Tarnoff, Scott, and Larry Nowels, *Foreign Aid: An Introductory Overview of U.S. Programs and Policy,* Congressional Research Service report (98-916), April, 15, 2004.

Thomas, Evan, *The Very Best Men, Four Who Dared: The Early Years of the CIA*, New York: Simon & Schuster, 1995.

Sosin, Gene, *Sparks of Liberty: An Insider's Memoir of Radio Liberty,* University Park, Pa.: Pennsylvania State University Press, 1999.

United Nations Development Programme, *Arab Human Development Report 2002: Creating Opportunities for Future Generations*, New York: United Nations Development Programme, 2002.

Warraq, Ibn, *Why I Am Not a Muslim*, Amherst, N.Y.: Prometheus, 1995.

———, *Leaving Islam: Apostates Speak Out*, Amherst, N.Y.: Prometheus, 2003.

Articles, Reports, Interviews, Web Pages, Etc.

Advisory Group on Public Diplomacy for the Arab and Muslim World, *Changing Minds, Winning Peace: A New Strategic Direction for U.S. Public Diplomacy in the Arab & Muslim World: Report of the Advisory Group on Public Diplomacy for the Arab and Muslim World, Submitted to the Committee on Appropriations, U.S. House of Representatives*, October 1, 2003.

Akkari, Ahmad, interview on *TV-Avisen*, Denmark Radio, April 2, 2006. Transcribed and translated at Web log "Agora." As of December 11, 2006: http://agora.blogsome.com/2006/04/03/demos-interview-with-naser-khader/).

"Al Azhar to Offer Courses in Thailand," *The Nation* (Bangkok), September 23, 2004.

al-Baghdadi, Ahmad, "Kuwati Progressive Scholar: 'All the Good Is in Secular Thought, All the Evil in Religious Thought,'" translated excerpts from articles appearing in the November 14, 2004, and November 16–17, 2004, editions of *Al-Siyassa*, Middle East Media Research Initiative Special Dispatch No. 823, December 3, 2004. As of December 11, 2006: http://memri.org/bin/articles.cgi?Page=archives&Area=sd&ID=SP82304

Allievi, Stefano, "Islam in Italy," in Shireen Hunter, ed., *Islam, Europe's Second Religion*, Westport and London: Praeger, 2002.

Al-Nabulsi, Shaker, "Arab Progressive: The Arabs Are Still Slaves to a Medieval Mentality," excerpts from an article published on www.rezgar.com, August 14, 2004, Middle East Research Institute Special Dispatch Series No. 786, September 20, 2004. As of December 11, 2006: http://memri.org/bin/articles.cgi?Page=archives&Area=sd&ID=SP78604

al-Qaradawi, Yusef, "Secularism vs. Islam," Web page, n.d. As of December 11, 2006: http://islamicweb.com/beliefs/cults/Secularism.htm

Anatol, Von, "Mit Gemäßigten Wie Diesen" ["With Moderates Like These"], *Die Gazette*, 23, December 2001. As of December 11, 2006: http://www.gazette.de/Archiv/Gazette-Dezember2001/Elyas.html

An-Naim, Abdullahi, "Public Forum on Human Rights, Religion & Secularism," notes made by Siew Foong on speech delivered by Abdullahi An-Naim, National Evangelical Christian Fellowship Malaysia, January 18, 2003. As of December 11, 2006:
http://www.necf.org.my/newsmaster.
cfm?&menuid=40&parentid=12&action=view&retrieveid=257

Aras, Bulent, and Omer Caha, "Fethullah Gulen and His Liberal 'Turkish Islam' Movement," *MERIA Journal*, Vol. 4, No. 4, December 2000. As of December 11, 2006:
http://meria.biu.ac.il/journal/2000/issue4/jv4n4a4.html

Arjomand, Homa, "International Declaration, Islamic Schools Should Be Banned, Children Have No Religion," petition, n.d. As of December 11, 2006: http://new.petitiononline.com/nofaith/petition.html

Asia Foundation, "The Asia Foundation: Bangladesh, Projects," Web page, n.d. As of December 11, 2006: http://www.asiafoundation.org/Locations/bangladesh_projects.html

———, "The Asia Foundation: Indonesia, Projects," Web page, n.d. As of December 11, 2006: http://www.asiafoundation.org/Locations/indonesia_projects.html

———, "The Asia Foundation: Overview," Web page, n.d. As of December 11, 2006: http://www.asiafoundation.org/Partnerships/overview.html

———, "Education Reform and Islam in Indonesia," pamphlet, n.d.

"Bahrain Women's Union Gets Ministry's Approval," *Khaleej Times,* July, 27, 2006. As of December 11, 2006: http://www.gulfinthemedia.com/index. php?id=230900&news_type=Political&lang=en&.

Bechari, Mohamed, "¿Qué lugar ocupará el Islam en la nueva Europa?" *Memoria,* No. 202, December 2005. As of December 11, 2006: http://memoria.com.mx/?q=node/699

Bencheikh, Soheib, "Islam and Secularism," interview by Liberal Islam Network, April 2004. As of December 11, 2006: http://www.qantara.de/webcom/show_article.php/_c-478/_nr-130/i.html

BMENA Foundation for the Future, "Mission and Mandate," Web page. As of December 11, 2006: http://www.bmenafoundation.org/mission.html

Braden, Tom, "I'm Glad the CIA Is 'Immoral,'" *Saturday Evening Post,* May 20, 1967.

British Muslim Forum, "BMF Objectives," Web page, n.d. As of December 11, 2006: http://www.bmf.eu.com/bmf_obj.php

Brody, John, "For Muslim Who Says Violence Destroys Islam, Violent Threats," *New York Times,* March 11 2006.

Brumberg, Daniel, "Islam Is Not *the* Solution (or *the* Problem)," *The Washington Quarterly,* Vol. 29, No. 1, Winter 2005–2006.

Carew, Anthony, "The American Labor Movement in Fizzland: The Free Trade Union Committee and the CIA", *Labour History,* Vol. 39, No. 4, February 1998.

———, "The Politics of Productivity and the Politics of Anti-Communism: American and European Labour in the Cold War," *Intelligence and National Security*, Vol. 18, No. 2, Summer 2003.

The Center for Islam and the Study of Democracy, *2004 President's Report*. As of May 2005:
http://www.islam-democracy.org

Center for Religious Freedom, *Saudi Publications on Hate Ideology Fill American Mosques*, Washington, D.C.: Freedom House, 2005. As of December 11, 2006:
http://www.freedomhouse.org/religion/publications/Saudi%20Report/FINAL%20FINAL.pdf

Centre for the Study of Society and Secularism, "About Us," Web page, n.d. As of December 11, 2006:
www.csss-isla.com/aboutus.php

Coleman, Sarah, "Shabana Rehman, Making Fun of the Mullahs," *World Press Review*, Vol. 9, No. 50, September 2003. As of December 11, 2006:
http://www.worldpress.org/Europe/1437.cfm

Council on Foreign Relations, "In Support of Arab Democracies: Why and How," Madeleine K. Albright and Vin Weber, co-chairs, Independent Task Force Report No. 54, 2005.

Dankowitz, A., "Arab Intellectuals: Under Threat by Islamists," Middle East Media Research Institute Inquiry and Analysis Series No. 254, November 23, 2005. As of December 11, 2006:
http://memri.org/bin/articles.cgi?Page=archives&Area=ia&ID=IA25405

"Der Multikulturalismus hat dem Scharia: Islam in Europa die Tür Geöffnet," *NZZ am Sontag*, October 2002. As of December 11, 2006:
http://www.aidlr.org/german/rte/files//BassamTibiOCR-2.pdf

"Editor's Arrest on Blasphemy Charges Highlights Difficulties Facing Journalists," *PakTribune Online*, October 23, 2005. As of December 11, 2006:
http://www.paktribune.com/news/index.php?id=123377

Elad-Altman, Israel, "Democratic Elections and the Egyptian Muslim Brotherhood," Hudson Institute, *Current Trends in Islamist Ideology*, Vol. 3, 2006.

Ellian, Afshin, "About Ashfin Ellian," Web log. As of December 11, 2006:
http://afshinellian.blogspot.com

"Excerpt from Minutes of Special Meeting of the Board of NCFE Directors," August 4, 1949, Box 286, Radio Free Europe Corporate Policy 1950–1956, Radio Free Europe/Radio Liberty Corporate Archives, Hoover Institution Archives.

European Students Forum–AEGEE, "EuroIslam," Web page, n.d. As of December 11, 2006:
http://www.karl.aegee.org/calendar/(ProjectDisplay)/EuroIslam?OpenDocument

Feder, Glen, "The Muslim Brotherhood in France," *In the National Interest*, Web site, September 21, 2005. As of December 11, 2006:
http://www.inthenationalinterest.com/Articles/September%202005/September2005Feder.html

Free-Minds.org, "The Shahada," Web page, n.d. As of December 11, 2006:
http://www.free-minds.org/articles/hadith/testimony.htm

Fuller, Graham "The Future of Political Islam," *Foreign Affairs*, Vol. 81, No. 2, March/April 2002. As of December 11, 2006:
http://www.foreignaffairs.org/20020301faessay7971/graham-e-fuller/the-future-of-political-islam.html

Glazov, Jamie, "The Anti-Terror, Pro-Israel Sheikh," interview with Sheikh Abdul Hadi Palazzi, *FrontPageMagazine.com*, September 12, 2005. As of December 11, 2006:
http://www.frontpagemagazine.com/Articles/ReadArticle.asp?ID=19444

"Gray Broadcasting Policy Toward the Soviet Union," May 1, 1958. Appendices to Memorandum for the President from the Director of Central Intelligence, declassified for Conference on Cold War Broadcasting Impact, Stanford, Calif., October 13–15, 2004, Document Reader.

Heggy, Tarek, "This House Believes in the Separation of Mosque and State," transcript of comments made during debate, Doha Debates, November 30, 2004. As of December 11, 2006:
http://www.thedohadebates.com/output/Page35.asp

Hendelman-Baavur, Liora, Nabila Espanioly, Eleana Gordon, Anat Lapidot-Firilla, Judith Colp Rubin, Sima Wali, "Women in the Middle East: Progress or Regress? A Panel Discussion" *MERIA Journal*, Vol. 10, No. 2, June 2006. As of December 11, 2006:
http://meria.idc.ac.il/journal/2006/issue2/Panel_Women.pdf

Heneghan, Tom, "Vienna Imam Says Yes to Europe, No to 'Euro-Islam,'" interview with Sheikh Adnan Ibrahim, Reuters, April 12, 2006, reprinted as "European Imam Conference Spells It Out—No to Euro-Islam, Yes to Islam in Europe," Web page, *Militant Islam Monitor*. As of December 11, 2006:
http://www.militantislammonitor.org/article/id/1831

Human Rights Watch, "Imprisoned Kuwaiti Scholar: Academics Demand Release," press release, Oct. 13, 1999. As of December 11, 2006:
http://www.hrw.org/press/1999/oct/kuwait.htm

———, "Saudi Arabia: Teachers Silenced on Blasphemy Charges," *Human Rights News*, November 17, 2005. As of December 11, 2006:
http://hrw.org/english/docs/2005/11/16/saudia12049.htm

Husna, Lilis N., interview in Ford Foundation, *Celebrating Indonesia: Fifty Years with the Ford Foundation, 1953–2003*, [Jakarta], 2003, p. 213. As of December

2006:
http://www.fordfound.org/elibrary/documents/5002/216.cfm#5002-div2-d0e8446

Ibn Rushd Fund for Freedom of Thought, "Who Are We?" Web page, n.d. As of
December 11, 2006:
http://www.ibn-rushd.org/pages/en

International Humanist and Ethical Union, "Younis Sheik Free," Web page,
January 23, 2004. As of December 11, 2006:
http://www.iheu.org/node/271

International Republican Institute, "Partners in Peace," Web page, n.d. As of
December 11, 2006:
http://www.iri.org/mena/pip.asp

"Islam in Europe: Political & Security Issues for Europe; Implications for the
United States," workshop, CNA Corporation's Center for Strategic Studies,
January 14, 2005.

Islamic Philosophy Online, "al-Kindi Site," Web page, n.d. As of December 11,
2006:
http://www.muslimphilosophy.com/kindi/index.html

Kicksola, Joseph N., "The Clash of Civilizations Within Islam: The Struggle
over the Qu'ran Between Muslim Democrats and Theocrats," Regent University,
Virginia Beach, Va., April 2006 (unpublished).

Kinnane, William, "Winning over the Muslim Mind," *The National Interest,*
Spring 2004.

Kopstein, Jeffrey, "The Transatlantic Divide over Democracy Promotion," *The
Washington Quarterly,* Vol. 29, No. 2, Spring 2006, p. 87.

Kosmin, Barry, Egon Mayer, and Ariela Keysar, *American Religious Identification
Survey, 2001,* New York: Graduate Center of the City University of New York,
2001. As of December 11, 2006:
http://www.gc.cuny.edu/faculty/research_studies/aris.pdf

Kotek, Joel, "Youth Organizations as a Battlefield in the Cold War," *Intelligence
and National Security,* Vol. 18, No. 2, Summer 2003.

Lee, Sue-Ann, "Managing the Challenges of Radical Islam: Strategies to Win the
Hearts and Minds of the Muslim World," seminar paper, John F. Kennedy School
of Government, Harvard University, April 1, 2003.

Leirvik, Oddbjørn, "Report from a Delegation Visit to Indonesia by the Oslo
Coalition of Freedom of Religion or Belief," July 29–August 11, 2002. As of
December 11, 2006:
http://www.oslocoalition.org/html/project_indonesia/indonesia_project_report.
html

Liberal Islam Network, "About Liberal Islam Network," Web page, n.d. As of December 11, 2006:
http://islamlib.com/en/aboutus.php

Liddle, R. William, "Piety and Pragmatism: New Patterns of Islamic Politics in Democratic Indonesia," *Piety and Pragmatism: Trends in Indonesian Islamic Politics*, Asia Program Special Report No. 110, Woodrow Wilson International Center for Scholars, April 2003. As of December 11, 2006:
http://www.wilsoncenter.org/topics/pubs/asiarpt_110.pdf

Lilly, Edward P., "The Development of American Psychological Operations, 1945–1951," December 19, 1951, Box 22, Records of the Psychological Strategy Board, Harry S. Truman Library.

Lockard, Joe, "Marcel Khalife and Blasphemy," *Bad Subjects*, Web site, December 19, 1999. As of December 11, 2006:
http://bad.eserver.org/editors/1999/1999-12-16.html

Lucas, W. Scott, "Beyond Freedom, Beyond Control: Approaches to Cultural and the State-Private Network in the Cold War," *Intelligence and National Security*, Vol. 18, No. 2, Summer 2003.

Martinez, Patricia, "Deconstructing Jihad: Southeast Asian Contexts," in Kumar Ramakrishna and See Seng Tan, eds., *After Bali: The Threat of Terrorism in Southeast Asia*, Singapore: Institute of Defence and Strategic Studies, Nanyang Technological University, 2003.

Matthews, John P.C., "The West's Secret Marshall Plan for the Mind," *International Journal of Intelligence and Counter Intelligence,* Vol. 16, No. 3, July–September 2003.

Medhurst, Martin J., "Eisenhower and the Crusade for Freedom: The Rhetorical Origins of a Cold War Campaign," *Presidential Studies Quarterly*, Vol. 27, Fall 1997.

"Memorandum on Baltic Committees," 29 November 1955, Box 154, Baltic Committees, Radio Free Europe/Radio Liberty Corporate Archives, Hoover Institution Archives.

Middle East Partnership Initiative, "Success Stories," Web page, n.d. As of December 11, 2006:
http://www.mepi.state.gov/c16050.htm

Miichi, Ken, "Islamic Movements in Indonesia," *IIAS Newsletter*, No. 32, November 2003. As of December 11, 2006:
http://www.iias.nl/iiasn/32/RR_islamic_youth_movements_in_indonesia.pdf

Milson, Meneham, "Reform vs. Islamism in the Arab World Today," Middle East Media Research Institute Special Report No. 34, September 15, 2004. As of December 11, 2006:
http://memri.org/bin/articles.cgi?Page=archives&Area=sr&ID=SR3404

"Moderate Danish Muslims Targets of Attacks and Death Threats," text of report by Danish *Politiken* Web site, BBC Worldwide Monitoring, November 22, 2004.

Monroe, William T., "NDI's Positive Role Highlighted," interview, May 13, 2006. As of December 11, 2006:
http://manama.usembassy.gov/bahrain/ambtrib00513.html

Munir, Lily, "In Search of a New Islamic Identity in Indonesia," presentation, The United States–Indonesia Society (USINDO) Conference, Washington, D.C., November 11, 2003.

Murray, Ralph, "Progress Report on the Work of the IRD," memorandum to Christopher Warner, March 21, 1950. Foreign Office 1110/359/PR110/5, Public Record Office, United Kingdom.

Muslim Council of Britain, "It Doesn't Add Up," Web log entry, October 29, 2005. As of December 11, 2006:
http://mcbwatch.blogspot.com

Muzaffar, Chandra, interview, *Frontline*, October 10, 2001. As of December 11, 2006:
http://www.pbs.org/wgbh/pages/frontline/shows/muslims/interviews/muzaffar.html

Namazie, Maryam, "Biography," Web page, n.d. As of December 11, 2006:
http://www.maryamnamazie.com/biography.html

National Committee for a Free Europe, *Excerpt from Minutes of Special Meeting of the Board of NCFE Directors,* Stanford, Calif.: Hoover Institution Archives, 1949.

National Democratic Institute, "Congress of Democrats from the Islamic World," *The Middle East and North Africa in Focus: Regional Initiatives,* [June 2004]. As of December 11, 2006:
http://www.accessdemocracy.org/library/1735_reg_infocus_060104.pdf

National Endowment for Democracy, *The Backlash Against Democracy Assistance: A Report Prepared by the National Endowment for Democracy for Senator Richard G. Lugar, Chairman, Committee on Foreign Relations, United States Senate,* Washington, D.C.: National Endowment for Democracy, June 8, 2006.

National Opinion Research Center, *General Social Surveys,* computer file, n.d. As of December 11, 2006:
http://www.norc.org/projects/gensoc.asp

National Security Council, "National Security Council Directive on Office of Special Projects," NSC 10/2, 18 June 1948, Record Group 273, Records of the National Security Council, NSC 10/2, National Archives and Records Administration.

Nazir, Sameena, "Challenging Inequality: Obstacles and Opportunities Towards Women's Rights in the Middle East and North Africa," in Women's Rights in the Middle East and North Africa, Washington, D.C.: Freedom House, 2005. As of

December 11, 2006:
http://www.freedomhouse.org/template.cfm?page=163

Nowels, Larry and Connie Veillette, *Restructuring U.S. Foreign Aid: The Role of the Director of Foreign Assistance*, Congressional Research Service report (RS22411), September 8, 2006.

Nowels, Larry, Connie Veillette, Susan B. Epstein, *Foreign Operations (House)/ State, Foreign Operations, and Related Programs (Senate): FY2007 Appropriations*, Congressional Research Service report (RL33420), May 25, 2006.

Office of the Undersecretary of Defense for Acquisition, Technology, and Logistics, *Report of the Defense Science Board Task Force on Strategic Communications*, September 2004.

Paget, Karen, "From Stockholm to Leiden: The CIA's Role in the Formation of the International Student Conference," *Intelligence and National Security*, Vol. 18, No. 2, Summer 2003.

Philippine Center for Islam and Democracy, "Southeast Asian Muslim Leaders and Scholars Convene on Islam & Democratization," *PCID Policy Report*, Vol. 1, Issue 3, December 2005.

Policy Planning Staff to National Security Council, "Organized Political Warfare," 4 May 1948, Record Group 273, Records of the National Security Council, NSC 10/2. National Archives and Records Administration.

Progressive Muslim Union, "PMU Statement of Principles," Web page, n.d. As of December 11, 2006:
http://www.pmuna.org/

Project MAPS and Zogby International, *American Muslim Poll 2004*, October 2004. As of December 11, 2006:
http://www.projectmaps.com/AMP2004report.pdf

Qenawi, Ayman, "Danish Muslims 'Internationalize' Anti-Prophet Cartoons," *IslamOnline.net*, November 18, 2005. As of December 11, 2006:
http://islamonline.net/English/News/2005-11/18/article02.shtml

Rabasa, Angel, "Islamic Education in Southeast Asia," in Hillel Fradkin, Husain Haqqani, and Eric Brown, eds., *Current Trends in Islamist Ideology*, Vol. 2, Washington, D.C.: Hudson Institute, 2005.

Rosenau, William, "Waging the War of Ideas," in *The McGraw-Hill Homeland Security Handbook*, David Kamien, ed., New York: McGraw-Hill, 2006. As of December 11, 2006:
http://www.rand.org/pubs/reprints/RP1218/

Rugh, William, "Fixing Public Diplomacy for Arab and Muslim Audiences," in Adam Garfinkle, ed., *A Practical Guide to Winning the War on Terrorism*, Stanford, Calif.: Hoover Institution Press, 2004.

Sa'id, Ali Ahmad (AKA Adonis), "Renowned Syrian Poet Adonis: The Arabs Are Extinct Like the Sumerians, Greeks and Pharaohs; If the Arabs Are So Inept They Cannot Be Democratic, External Intervention Will Not Make Them So," excerpts from an interview with Ali Ahmad Sa'id on Dubai TV, March 11, 2006, translated, *Middle East Media Research Institute Special Dispatch Series*, No. 1121, March 21, 2006. As of December 11, 2006:
http://memri.org/bin/articles.cgi?Page=archives&Area=sd&ID=SP112106

Scott-Smith, Giles, "A Radical Democratic Political Offensive: Melvin J. Lasky, *Der Monat*, and the Congress of Cultural Freedom," *Journal of Contemporary History*, Vol. 35, No. 2, 2000.

———, "The Congress for Cultural Freedom, the End of Ideology and the 1955 Milan Conference: Defining the Parameters of Discourse," *Journal of Contemporary History*, Vol. 37, No. 3, 2002.

Shahrour, Muhammad, "The Divine Text and Pluralism in Muslim Societies," *Muslim Political Report*, No. 14, July/August 1997.

Sharp, Jeremy M., *U.S. Democracy Promotion Policy in the Middle East: The Islamist Dilemma*, Congressional Research Service report (RL33486), June 15, 2006.

Smith, Lee, "The Kiss of Death?" *Slate,* Nov. 24, 2004. As of December 11, 2006:
http://www.slate.com/id/2110126

"Sociedad Mundial del 'Dawa al-islamiyya,'" Web page, May 2, 2003. As of December 11, 2006:
http://www.webislam.com/numeros/2003/209/noticias/sociedad_mundial_dawa_islamiyya.htm

Statistics Netherlands, *Statline*, electronic database, 2005.

Stern, Sol, "A Short Account of International Student Politics, and the Cold War with Particular Reference to the NSA, CIA, etc.," *Ramparts,* Vol. 5, No. 9, March 1967.

United States–Indonesia Society, "Muslim Civil Society," Web page, n.d. As of April 26, 2005:
http://www.usindo.org/Briefs/2005/Robin%Bush.htm

———, "Muslim Society and Democracy," report on presentation, Washington, D.C., April 26, 2005. As of December 11, 2006:
http://www.usindo.org/Briefs/2005/Robin%20Bush.htm

U.S. Department of Defense, *Quadrennial Defense Review Report*, February 6, 2006, pp. 21–22. As of December 11, 2006:
http://www.defenselink.mil/qdr/report/Report20060203.pdf.

U.S. Department of State, *Counter Soviet Threats to the United States Security,* General Records of the Department of State, Records of the Policy Planning Staff 1947–1953. National Archives and Record Administration.

————, "FY 2007 International Affairs (Function 150) Budget Request," February 6, 2006. As of December 11, 2006:
http://www.state.gov/s/d/rm/rls/iab/2007/html/60200.htm

————, "Libya: Country Reports on Human Rights Practices, 2005," Web page, March 8, 2006. As of December 11, 2006:
http://www.state.gov/g/drl/rls/hrrpt/2005/61694.htm

U.S. Government Accountability Office, *Foreign Assistance: Middle East Partnership Initiative Offers Tools for Supporting Reform but Project Monitoring Needs Improvement*, GAO-05-711, August 2005.

————, *U.S. Public Diplomacy: State Department Efforts to Engage Muslim Audiences Lack Certain Communications Elements and Face Persistent Challenges*, GAO-06-535, Washington, D.C.: May 3, 2006.

Wahid, Abdurrahman, "Right Islam vs. Wrong Islam," *The Wall Street Journal*, December 30, 2005. As of December 11, 2006:
http://www.libforall.org/news-WSJ-right-islam-vs.-wrong-islam.html

Warner, Michael, "Origins of the Congress of Cultural Freedom 1949–1950," *Studies in Intelligence*, Vol. 38, No. 5, 1995.

————, "Sophisticated Spies: CIA's Links to Liberal Anti-Communists 1949–1967," *International Journal of Intelligence and Counter Intelligence*, Vol. 9, No. 4, Winter 1996/1997.

The White House, "Fact Sheet: The President's National Security Strategy," press release, March 16, 2006. As of December 11, 2006:
http://www.whitehouse.gov/news/releases/2006/03/20060316.html

Wise, Lindsay, "Show Them the Money: Why Is an American Program Aimed at Supporting Reform in the Arab World Coming Under Attack by Its Own Beneficiaries?" *Cairo Magazine*, July 25, 2005. As of December 11, 2006:
http://www.cairomagazine.
com/?module=displaystory&story_id=1231&format=html

Wittes, Tamara Cofman, "The Promise of Arab Liberalism," *Policy Review*, July 2004; or Amy Hawthorne, "The Middle East Partnership Initiative: Questions Abound," *Arab Reform Bulletin*, Vol. 1, No. 3, September 2003.